100 New
Bobbin Lace Patterns

Yusai Fukuyama

100 New Bobbin Lace Patterns

Yusai Fukuyama

B.T. Batsford Ltd • London

First published 1996
Reprinted 1997

Patterns designed by Yusai Fukuyama.
Illustrated and photographed by Yusai
Fukuyama.
Worked by Horikoshi Yayoi, Nojima Tomoyo,
       Tamagaki Minako, Takagi Sanae,
       Nakamura Akie and Sasaki Yasuko.
English text by Yasai Fukuyama.

© Yusai Fukuyama

Printed and bound in Great Britain by
Butler & Tanner Ltd, Frome and London.

Published by
B.T. Batsford Ltd
583 Fulham Road
London SW6 5BY

A catalogue record for this book is available
from the British Library

ISBN 0 7134 7370 3

Contents

Contents

Introduction

This book has been written for the bobbin lacemaker who has a grasp of the basic techniques, and as a source book of stitches and tips to enable more inventive lacemakers to create their own designs.

The designs used are freer than with traditional lace. The general rules need to be adapted to suit the particular pattern being worked.

There can be more than one way of working certain parts of the patterns. Small motifs are set out to guide the beginner through the basic lacemaking techniques and the working of a practice braid of stitches. This is followed by general introductions with guidance on starting and finishing the lace. The lacemaker will find it useful to refer to these later. Easy patterns are included as an exercise in one or more techniques of bobbin lace and are intended to take the lace-maker a step further.

By working systematically through the patterns, the lace-maker will acquire a real understanding of the lace and develop an ability to recognize and work the components of more complicated patterns. Some patterns without instructions are also included to provide further practice and interest as the lacemaker becomes more proficient.

I would like to express my sincere appreciation and thanks to my lace teacher, Mrs Elsie Luxton MBE, who has given me much advice and encouragement. I would also like to thank the museum staff who enabled me to study the lace in their collections. Finally, I would like to thank all my friends in the lace world for their friendship.

I hope this book will help and encourage all lacemakers and give as much pleasure to those making the designs as I had in producing them.

Einleitung

Dieses Buch wurde nicht nur für diejenigen Klöpplerinnen geschrieben, die bereits über Grundkenntnisse verfügen; es wird auch den Phantasiebegabten beim Entwurf eigener Kreationen als Handbuch für Muster und Tips dienen.

Die gezeigten Entwürfe sind freier gestaltet als die traditionellen Spitzenmuster, und aus diesem Grunde sind die allgemeinen Regeln dem zu klöppelnden Modell anzupassen.

Es kann bei einigen Teilen der Modelle vorkommen, dass mehrere Ausführungsmöglichkeiten bestehen. Kleine Motive sind für die Anfängerin bestimmt, um sie mit den Grundtechniken bekannt zu machen und ihr das Einüben verschiedener Muster zu erlauben. Allgemeine Ratschläge, auf die sie später zurückkommen kann, sollen der Klöpplerin helfen, eine Spitze zu beginnen und zu beenden. Damit sie Fortschritte machen kann, sind einfache Modelle als Übung in einer oder mehreren Techniken vorgesehen.

Beim Durcharbeiten der Muster wird die Klöpplerin zu einem tieferen Verständnis gelangen und die Fähigkeit entwickeln, die Besonderheiten schwieriger Muster zu erkennen und auszuführen. Einige Modelle sind zur Übung ohne Anleitung dargeboten, um Interesse zu wecken und weitere Fortschritte zu ermöglichen.

Bei dieser Gelegenheit möchte ich meiner Lehrerin, Frau Elsie Luxton MBE, für ihre zahlreichen Ratschläge und freundliche Ermunterung meine Anerkennung und meinen Dank aussprechen. Mein Dank richtet sich auch an das Museumspersonal, das mir erlaubte, die Spitzen ihrer Kollektionen einzusehen. Abschliessend möchte ich allen meinen Klöppelbekanntschaften für ihre Freundschaft danken.

Inleiding

Dit boek is geschreven voor de kantkloss(t)er, die de basis-
technieken beheerst, en als bronnenboek voor slagen en tips,
om meer creatieve kantkloss(t)ers te helpen hun eigen
ontwerpen te maken.

De ontwerpen zijn vrijer gebruitk dan in traditionele kant. De
algemene regels dienen te worden aangepast aan het patroon
dat men klost.

Sommige delen van de patronen kunnen op veschillende
manieren worden gewerkt. Om de beginner in de basis-
technieken te begeleiden, zijn kleine motiefjes en een
oefenband met slagen gegeven. Hierna volgen algemene
instructies over beginnen en eindigen van de kant. Als
oefening in een of meer kantklostechnieken en om de
kantkloss(t)er een stap verder te brengen, zijn eenvoudige
patronen bijgevoegd.

Door systematisch door de patronen heen te werken, zal de
kantkloss(t)er inzicht in de kant krijgen en kundigheid
ontwikkelen om delen van ingewikkelder patronen te herken-
nen en te klossen. Er zijn ook patronen zonder instructie
gegeven, voor meer oefening en interesse als de
kantkloss(t)er meer vaardigheid krijgt.

Ik wil mijn oprechte waardering en dank betuigen aan
mijn lerares, Mrs Elsie Luxton MBE, die me veel advies en
aanmoediging heeft gegeven. Ik wil ook het museum-
personeel bedanken, dat me de kant in hun collecties liet
bestuderen. Tenslotte dank ik al mijn vrienden in de
kantwereld, voor hum vriendschap.

Ik hoop dat dit boek alle kantkloss(t)ers zal helpen en hun
evenveel plezier zal geven tijdens het klossen van de
ontwerpen als ik had bij het tekenen er van.

Introduction

Ce livre a été écrit à l'attention de la dentellière désirant approfondir ses connaissances des techniques de base et servira également à celle qui arrive au stade de la création, comme un recueil de points et d'astuces pour inventer ses propres ouvrages.

Les dessins présentés sont d'une conception plus libre que la dentelle traditionnelle. Les règles de principe doivent donc être adaptées au modèle particulier à exécuter.

Certaines parties des modèles présentent plusieurs possibilités d'exécution. De petits motifs sont conçus de façon à guider la débutante dans les techniques de base et lui permettre de s'entraîner pour différents points. Ceci est complété par des indications générales pour aider la dentellière à commencer et à terminer une dentelle. Elle pourra s'y référer plus tard. Pour faciliter les progrès, des modèles sans difficultés sont inclus pour servir comme exercises dans une ou plusieurs techniques de dentelle.

En exécutant systématiquement ces modèles, la dentellière arrivera à une compréhension approfondie de la dentelle et developpera sa capacité à reconnaître et à faire les différents éléments d'un modèle plus compliqué.

Pour amener la dentellière à une recherche et à un intérêt accrus au fur et à mesure de ses progrès, certains modèles sont présentés sans instructions particulières.

J'aimerais exprimer mon estime sincère et ma gratitude à mon professeur de dentelle, Madame Elsie Luxton MBE qui m'a beaucoup guidée et encouragée. Mes remerciements s'addressent également au personnel de musée qui m'a permis d'étudier les dentelles de leurs collections. Enfin, je voudrais remercier pour leur amitié tous mes amis dans le monde de la dentelle.

J'espère que ce livre aidera et encouragera toutes les dentellières et donnera aux créatrices autant de plaisir que j'ai ressenti moi-même en créant ces modèles.

はじめに

ここにご紹介するパターンは、やさしい初心者用のものから、多少手の込んだものまでであります。

この本は、ボビンレースの基礎知識を持つ方と、創意工夫なさろうとする方にも、技術やコツが将来ご自分のデザインを創作される折に役立つよう心がけました。

この本のデザインは伝統的なレースよりも、むしろ自由なスタイルをとっております。

一般的な技術を、これらの作品を制作するにあたり、応用しています。

パターンのどの部分も、必ず一つの方法しかないと限定するものではありません。

小さなモティーフは、初心者の方に基礎知識と様々な織り方が練習出来るようにしてあります。

織り始めの方法と、まとめ方の一般的な練習も兼ねております。

これらの各種基礎技術は、将来きっと役にたつものと思います。

やさしいパターンにでも、一つか二つのボビンレースの技法が含まれています。

そして、その練習は、技術を更に一段階上達させることでしょう。

パターンを系統だてて学ぶことにより、レースを確実に理解できますし、可能性を発見し、更に手の込んだパターンも、こなすことが出来るようになります。

尚、この本のパターンの幾つかは、型紙と写真のみで、解説がついていないものも含まれています。

これらは、更に練習して、熟達して頂くための、研究用として加えたものです。

最後になりますが、貴重なご助言と、おしみない励ましを頂きましたエルシー・ラクストン先生に、心より御礼申し上げます。

そして、博物館の学芸員の方々のご厚意により、貴重な資料の数々を拝見できる機会を得ることができましたことも、忘れることが出来ません。

レースを通して知り合った、世界各地の友人たちの、温かい友情にも、心から感謝致します。

この本が、レース作りを楽しむのに、お役に立つことができれば幸いです。

How to use this book

This book has been planned so that a lacemaker with a basic knowledge of bobbin lacemaking can easily understand the patterns by studying the diagrams and photographs. As there is very little written description with the patterns, it is anticipated that language will not be a barrier and hence the book may be used by lacemakers in any country, irrespective of the language they use.

When making the motif, the lacemaker is looking at the wrong side of the work. So the lacemaker needs to reverse the photograph of the finished lacework in their mind. It is not an easy task for the lacemaker. Lacemakers are recommended to use a small hand mirror to find the same direction and figure from the photograph of the finished lacework. Refer to appendix page 134, diagram 237.

All patterns have been worked in cotton crochet thread, D.M.C. Cordonnet Special No. 70. The size of the thread can be altered according to the availability of the personnel selection of the lacemaker. The size of the pricking can also be altered by using the enlargement or reduction facility available on most photocopiers. The thread must then be selected to suit the size to be worked.

All prickings are shown in the actual size.

Anmerkungen zum Gebrauch dieses Buches

Dieses Buch wurde so entworfen, dass die Klöpplerin mit Grundkenntnissen ohne Schwierigkeiten die Modelle beim Betrachten der Diagramme und Fotos verstehen kann. Sehr wenig Text begleitet die Muster, so dass die Sprache keine Barriere darstellt und das Buch von Klöpplerinnen aller Länder ohne Rüchsicht auf die Landessprache verstanden werden kann.

Beim Klöppeln betrachtet die Klöpplerin die Rückseite der Spitze. Deshalb muss sie das Foto, das die Schauseite zeigt, in ihrer Vorstellung umkehren. Das ist nicht ganz einfach. Die Klöpplerin sollte deshalb einen kleinen Taschenspiegel benutzen, um im Vergleich mit dem Foto der fertigen Spitze die gleiche Richtung und das gleiche Bild zu erhalten. Siehe dazu den Anhang auf Seite 134, Diagramm 237.

Alle Muster wurden mit D.M.C. Baumwollhäkelgarn "Cordonnet Special" Nr. 70 gearbeitet. Die Stärke des Garns kann je nach Verfügbarkeit oder der persönlichen Wahl der Klöpplerin abgeändert werden. Auch der gestochene Klöppelbrief ist mit einem Fotokopierer leicht zu vergrössern oder zu reduzieren, wobei das Garn der Grösse der Spitze angepasst werden muss.

Alle gestochenen Klöppelbriefe sind in Naturgrösse gezeigt.

Hoe dit boek te gebruiken

Dit boek is zo opgezet, dat een kankloss(t)er met basiskennis de patronen makkelijk kan begrijpen door de werktekeningen en foto's te bekijken. Aangezien er weinig geschreven instructie is bij de patronen, zal taal geen probleem zijn, en dus kan het boek gebruikt worden door kantkloss(t)ers uit alle landen, welke taal zij ook spreken.

Tijdens het klossen van een motief, kijkt men op de achterkant van het werk. De kantkloss(t)er dient dus in gedachten de foto van de kant om te draaien. Dat is niet eenvoudig. Ik adviseer daarom een spiegeltje te gebruiken om dezelfde richting en vorm te vinden als op de foto. Zie aanhangsel pagina 134, werktekening 237.

Alle patronen zijn geklost met katoenen haakgaren, D.M.C. Cordonnet Special nr 70. De dikte van het garen kan gewijzid worden naar persoonlijke keuze van de kantkloss(t)er. De grootte van de prikking kan ook worden veranderd met de vergrotings- of verkleiningsmogelijkheden van de meeste copieerapparaten. Dan moet ook de gardendikte worden aangepast.

Alle prikkingen zijn gegeven in de werkelijke grootte.

Comment utiliser ce livre

Ce livre a été conçu de façcon à permettre à la dentellière possédant une connaisance de base de la dentelle aux fuseaux, de comprendre facilement les modèles présentés en regardant les dessins et les photos. Très peu de descriptions écrites accompagnent les modèles afin que la langue ne s'impose pas comme une barrière. C'est la raison pour laquelle ce livre peut être utile aux dentellières de tous les pays, indépendamment de leur langue.

Au cours de l'exécution d'un modèle, la dentellière regarde toujours l'envers de son ouvrage. Elle doit donc s'imaginer inversée la photo qui représente l'ouvrage terminé. Evidemment, ceci n'est pas une tâche facile. Nous recommandons aux dentellières d'utiliser un petit miroir de poche pour trouver la même orientation et représentation sur la photo de l'ouvrage fini. Voir annexe page 134, dessin 237.

Tous les modèles sont exécutés en fil coton pour crochet D.M.C. Cordonnet Spécial no. 70. La dentellière peut choisir un fil de grosseur différente selon la disponibilité ou son choix personnel. Le piquage est à agrandir ou à réduire en utilisant une photocopieuse appropriée. Dans ce cas, le fil doit être choisi en fonction de la grandeur de la dentelle à exécuter.

Tous les piquages sont présentés en grandeur naturelle.

この本の使い方

この本は、ボビンレースの基礎知識をお持ちの方が、解説図と写真を丁寧に学習することにより、パターンをやさしく理解出来るように工夫してあります。
パターンには、説明が余り多くありませんが、わかりやすい図を沢山つけることにより、世界各地でいかなる言語を使う方でも、容易に理解できるように努めました。

レースのモティーフを織るときは、レースの裏を見て制作することになります。
その為、レースの完成写真と、制作中のレースを見比べる時には、写真を頭の中で裏返さなければなりません。レースの向きを逆に想像するのは、なかなかやさしいことではありません。小さな手鏡を通して、レースの完成写真をご覧になって下さい。
ピローの上で、制作中のレースと、同じ向きになる筈です。
後ろの 134 ページの図 237 を参考になさって下さい。

この本の作品を作るのにDMCの綿レース糸の70番を使用致しました。
全作品共、70番使用です。

お作りになる方の好みにより、糸の太さを変えることも出来ます。
フォトコピーの機械で、拡大したり、縮小したりしてみて下さい。
但し、糸の太さも変わってきますので、拡大、又は、縮小した型紙にふさわしい太さを、お選び下さい。

手順が分かりやすいように、解説図を用意しました。
制作順序は数字で、そして、制作する方向は矢印で示しました。

この本では、全部実物大型紙をつけてあります。

日本語によるボビンレースの本が、NHK出版より出ております。
福山有彩著「ボビンレース」の本も、是非、参考になさって下さい。

Yusai Fukuyama's Patterns

1. Bear

Start from 1 with 4 pairs.
For working shirt add 6 more pairs.

Introducing whole-stitch trail,
leaf, plait, start and finish.

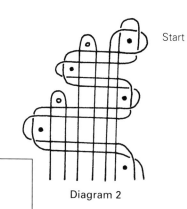

Start

Diagram 2

○ Temporary pin
This symbol indicates a temporary pinhole
to be used until work has begun. Do not
forget to remove as soon as possible.

Working order and direction

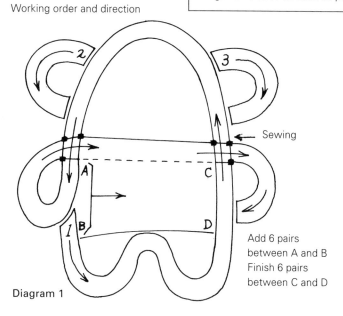

Sewing

Diagram 1

Add 6 pairs
between A and B
Finish 6 pairs
between C and D

Start line for process 2: 4 pairs

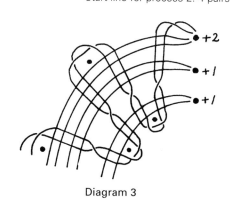

● +2

● +1

● +1

Diagram 3

Figure 1

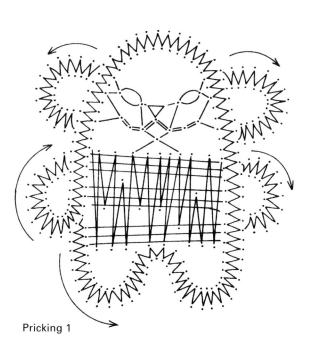

Pricking 1

Face

Start from bottom of nose at A with 6 pairs.
(See diagram 5).

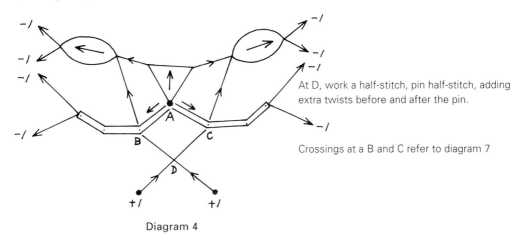

At D, work a half-stitch, pin half-stitch, adding extra twists before and after the pin.

Crossings at a B and C refer to diagram 7

Diagram 4

Nose

Start with 6 pairs.
Make a triangular tally.

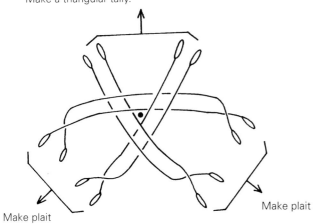

Make plait

Make plait

Make plait

Diagram 5

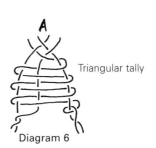

Triangular tally

Diagram 6

Crossing plait and a pair.

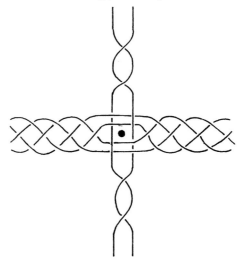

Diagram 7

○ **Temporary pin**
This symbol indicates a temporary pinhole to be used until work has begun. Do not forget to remove as soon as possible.

2. Rabbit

Start from 1 with 4 pairs and make the body.
Then make stomach with 4 pairs, twisting weavers
between each whole-stitch with the passive pairs. Add
extra twists when weavers are taken out to sew into body.

How to start part 1 and part 2.

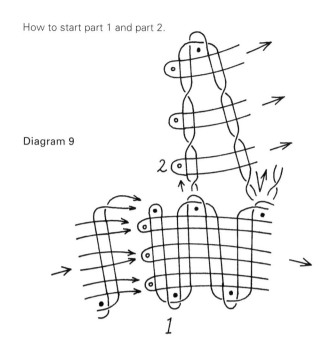

Diagram 9

Working order and direction

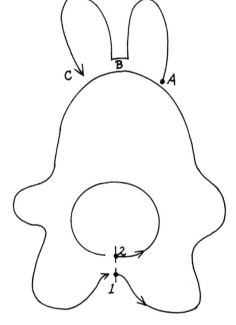

Diagram 8

○ Temporary pin (refer to page 18)

Figure 2

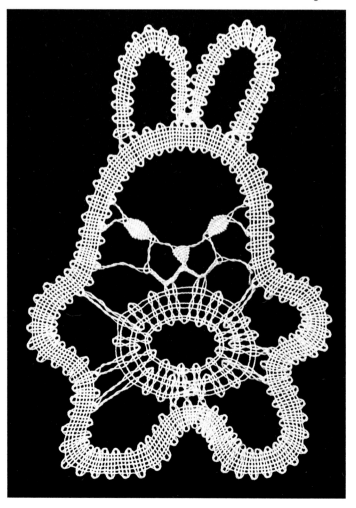

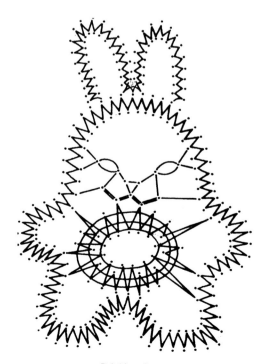

Pricking 2

Face

Start from bottom of nose at A with 6 pairs.
(Refer to diagram 5, page 19).

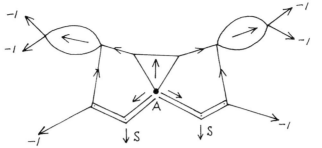

S: Sewing to stomach

Diagram 10

Make a triangular tally
at A

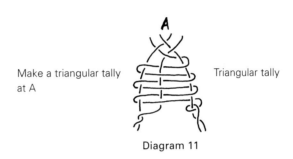

Triangular tally

Diagram 11

Ears

Start from A with 4 pairs.
Change the direction at B and finish at C.

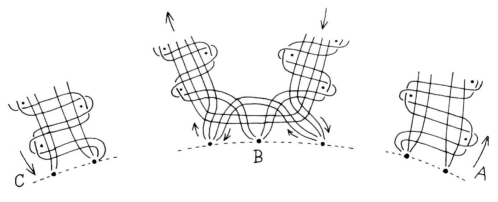

Diagram 14　　　　　Diagram 13　　　　　Diagram 12

3. Pony

Work the shape of the pony
in whole-stitch with 4 pairs.

At sharp curved places like the mouth
and tail, change weaver and inner passives.
(Refer to diagram 19). A separate diagram
(diagram 17) is given for the ear.

Complete the outer shape first
then the inner filling.

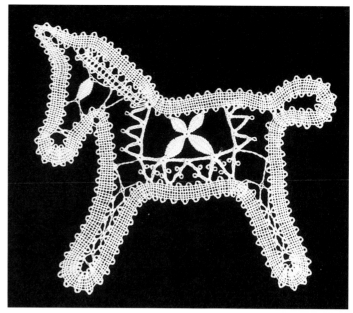

Figure 3

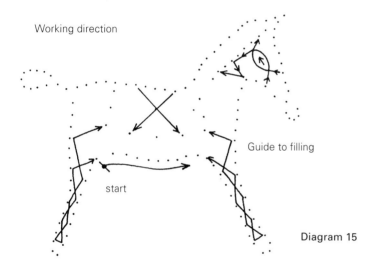

Working direction

Guide to filling

start

Diagram 15

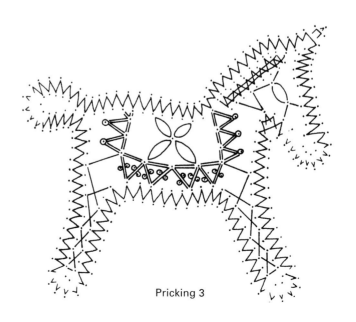

Pricking 3

Windmill

Ingenious method of joining
2 sets of 2 pairs round a pin

Guide to working the ear

Windmill crossing

Diagram 16

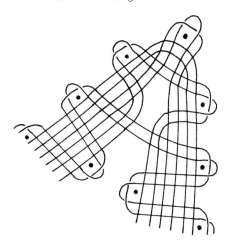

Diagram 17

Turn the corner sharply

Work the section of the mane,
then continue to plait. Small lines
indicate twists.

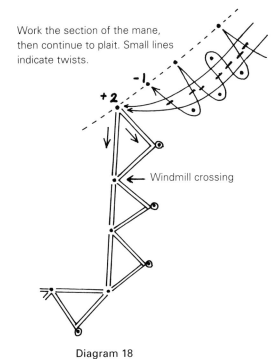

Windmill crossing

Diagram 18

Curved Trail

Leave the worker at inner edge and
take inner passives as a new worker

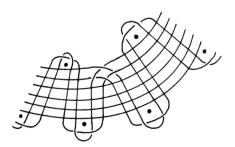

Diagram 19

4. Tropical Fish

Work trail in whole-stitch with 4 pairs.

Complete the shape first, then the filling.

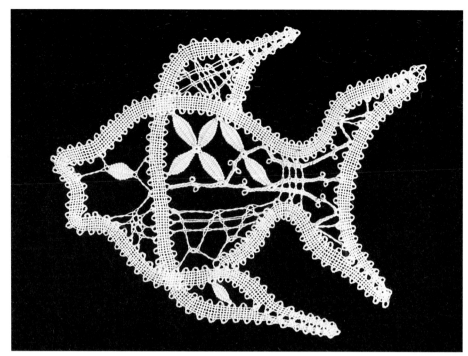

Figure 4

Guide to turning the point of the tail.

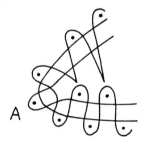

Diagram 21

Working direction

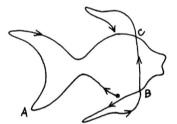

Diagram 20

Crossing over previously made braid

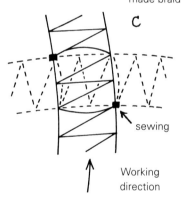

sewing

Working direction

Diagram 23
Guide to working at C

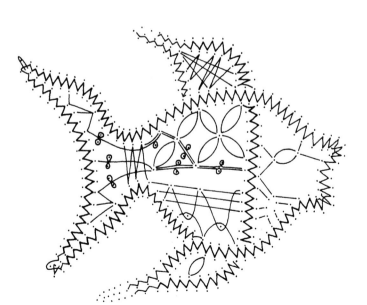

Pricking 4

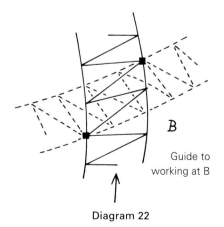

B

Guide to working at B

Diagram 22

5. Little Bird

Start at base of tail twisting once between whole-stitch passives. Place edge pin inside 2 pairs. When tail is complete, remove one pair of passives and change to whole-stitch braid.

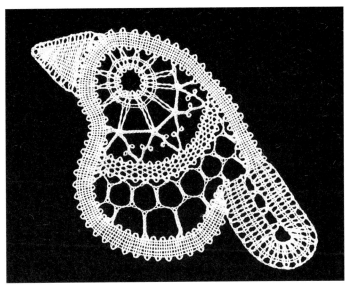

Figure 5

Working order and direction

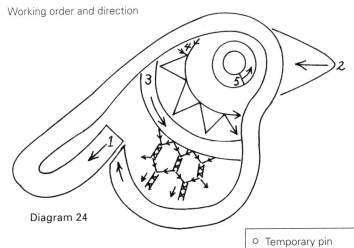

Diagram 24

o Temporary pin (refer to page 18).

Guide to adding a new pair.

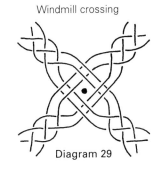

Diagram 27   Diagram 28

Windmill crossing

Diagram 29

Pricking 5

Diagram 25

Guide to setting and making beak.

Setting 4 pairs at the top pin.

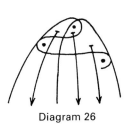

Diagram 26

Adding a new pair.

Note
Pairs are indicated by single lines.

6. Shell

Start with 4 pairs

Add two more pairs to where braid widens, removing them after twisted area narrows and reverts to whole-stitch.

Working order and direction

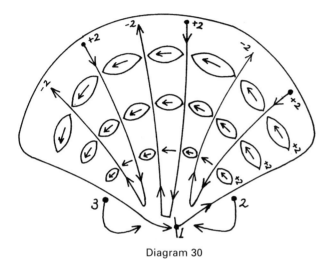

Diagram 30

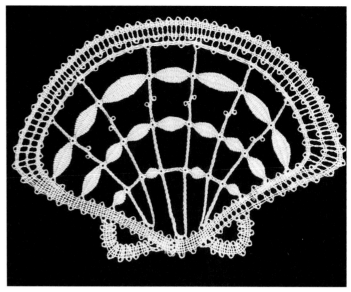

Figure 6

Guide to crossing plait and leaf.

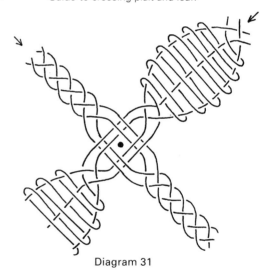

Diagram 31

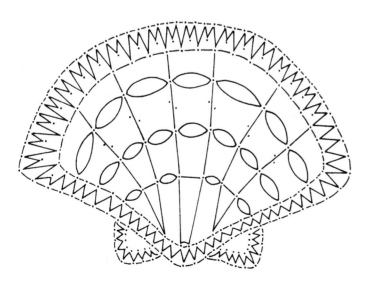

Pricking 6

7. Dolphin

Start with 4 pairs in whole-stitch braid. For a guide
to turning at the points of the dorsal fin and tail,
see diagram 33.

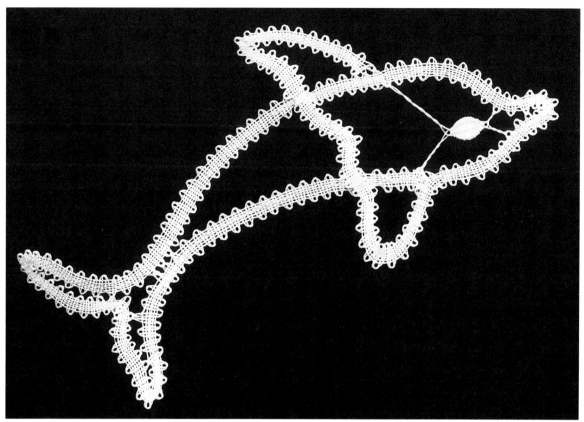

Figure 7

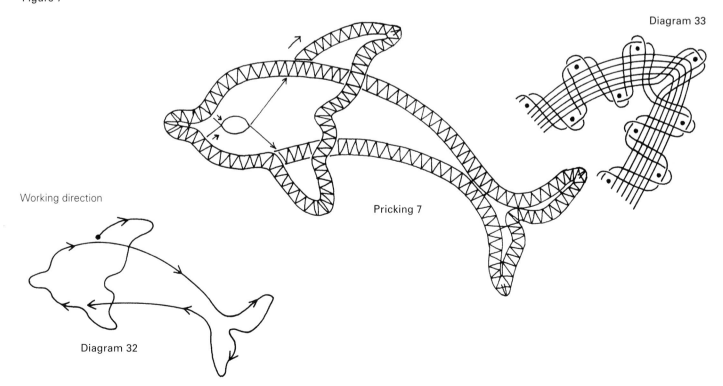

Diagram 33

Pricking 7

Working direction

Diagram 32

8. Butterfly-1

Start at 1 (diagram 34) with 4 pairs in a whole-stitch braid, adding twists as shown in figure 8.

After completing the outer shape, fill the space with leaves and plaits.

For guide to crossing two leaves or two plaits, refer to page 134 (windmill crossing), diagram 234.

Leaf: page 134, diagram 236.

Plait the antenna with two pairs.

Figure 8

Pricking 8

Working order and direction

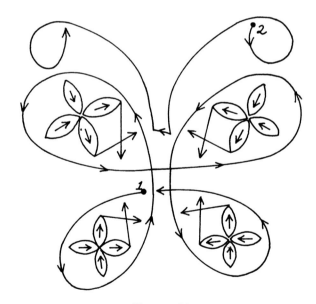

Diagram 34

Filling:
Windmill crossing of two leaves and two plaits.

9. Chick

Outline is worked in a whole-stitch
braid with twisted weaver using
4 pairs.

Sections 1-5: 4 pairs
Section 6: 7 pairs
Work in half-stitch with whole-stitch
and twist before and after each pin.
Eye: 2 pairs
Beak: 4 pairs

Figure 9

Working order and direction

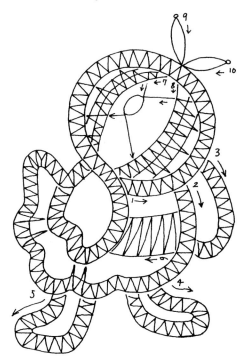

Pricking 9

Guide to starting beak.
Set in two pairs at pin 9
Twist 3 times and make a leaf.
Repeat at pin 10.
Leaf: refer to page 134,
diagram 236.

10. Apple

Start with 5 pairs for apple,
7 pairs for the leaf section.

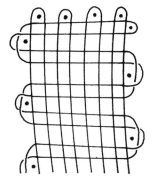

Diagram 35

Set in 3 pairs at the top pin of leaf.

Diagram 37

Diagram 38

Finishing apple section.

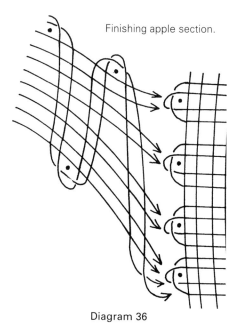

Diagram 36

Showing beginning part of leaf.

Diagram 39

Working order and direction

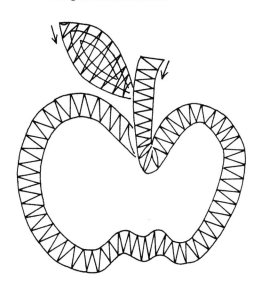

Pricking 10

Figure 10

11. Pear

Setting in 5 pairs at the tip of the leaf.

Pear: 5 pairs.
Leaf: 9 pairs.

Diagram 40

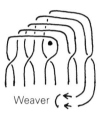

Take right pair
as a weaver.

Weaver

Diagram 41

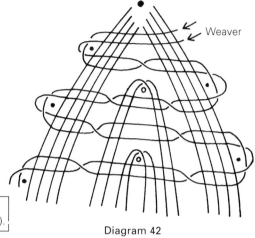

Weaver

Diagram 42

○ Temporary pin
(refer to page 18).

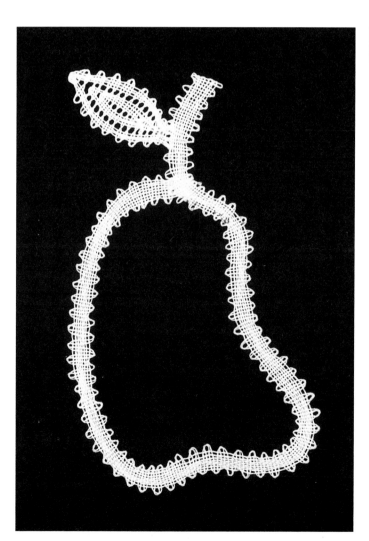

Figure 11

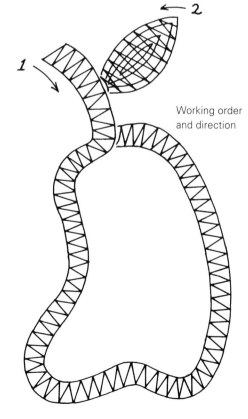

Working order
and direction

Pricking 11

31

12. Strawberry

First section: 4 pairs.
Filling: 4 pairs.
Second section: 2 pairs plaited.

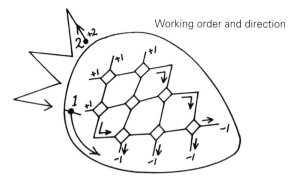

Working order and direction

Diagram 43

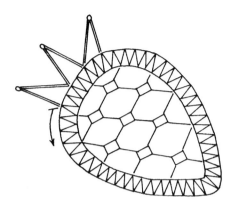

Pricking 12

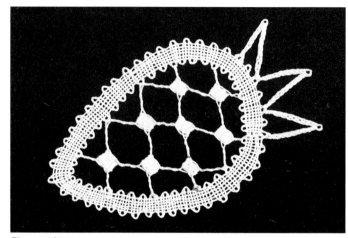

Figure 12

13. Maple Leaf

Continuous whole-stitch braid
with 4 pairs

Working direction

Diagram 44

Figure 13

Guide showing the points
and angle of leaf.

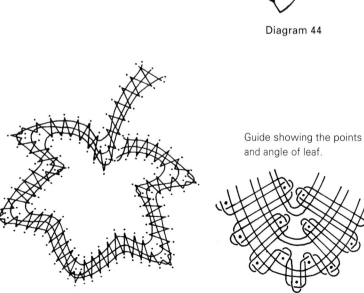

Pricking 13

Diagram 45

14. Flower-1

Continuous whole stitch braid
with 4 pairs.

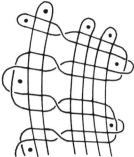

Guide to setting in
and working the
first section.

Diagram 47

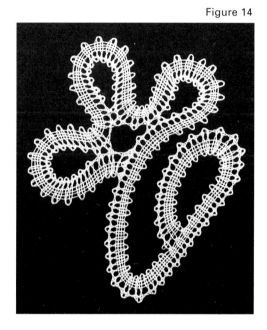

Figure 14

Working direction

Diagram 46

Pricking 14

15. Butterfly-2

Working direction

Diagram 48

Diagram 49

Guide to setting in
and working the
first section.

Figure 15

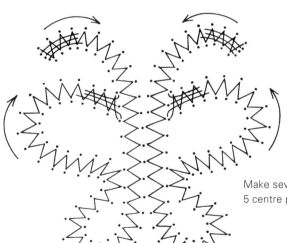

Make sewings at
5 centre pins.

Pricking 15

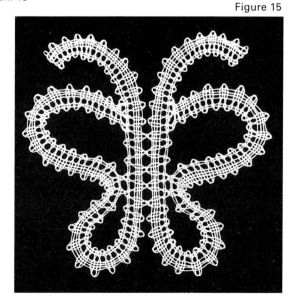

33

16. Flower-2

Continuous whole stitch braid
with 4 pairs.

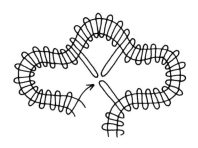

Diagram 51

Working direction

Diagram 50

Sewing and joining 3 loops at the central pinhole.

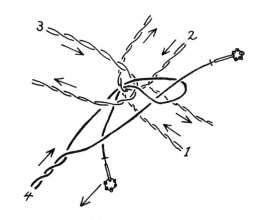

Diagram 52

Figure 16

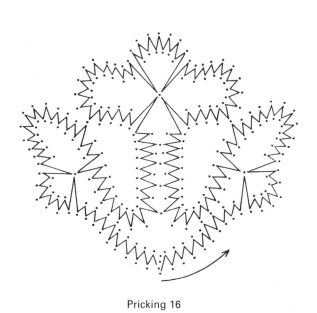

Pricking 16

17. Motif-1

Inner ring: 4 pairs. From mark * take weaver and inner passives and make a plait for diamond filling (diagram 54).

Diagram 53

Figure 17

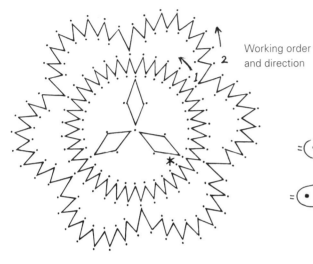

Working order and direction

Pricking 17

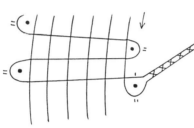

Diagram 54

Starting plait

Diagram 55

18. Motif-2

Start with 6 pairs.
Inner part: crossing 2 plaits, plait and leaf.
Refer to page 134, windmill crossing.

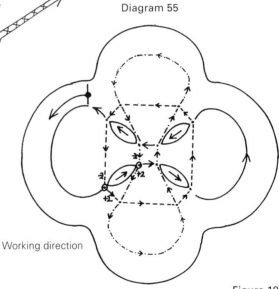

Working direction

Figure 18

Pricking 18

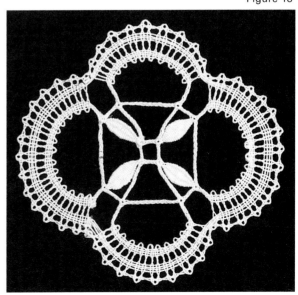

19. Motif-3

Inner ring: 4 pairs.
Flower petals and leaves: 8 pairs.
Outer ring of plaits is decorated with picots.

Working order and direction   Figure 19

Pricking 19

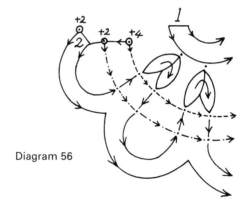

Diagram 56

20. Star-1

Set 4 pairs at
mark ⊙. Make
shape with 2
plaits. Refer to
windmill cross-
ing page 134;
then fill 4 leaves.

Working direction

Figure 20

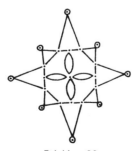

Pricking 20

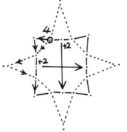

Diagram 57

21. Star-2

Set in 4 pairs to make 2 plaits. A further 2 pairs are needed for 2 plaits indicated by dotted lines.

Working direction

Windmill crossing. Refer to page 134.

Figure 21

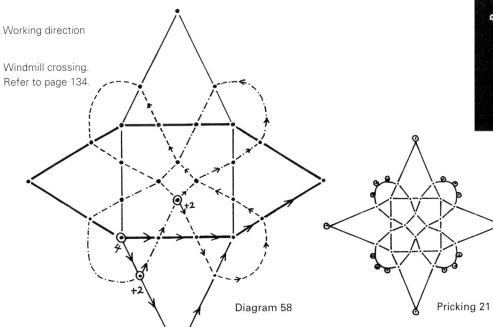

Diagram 58

Pricking 21

22. Little Heart

Heart: 4 pairs

Guide to showing the point of the heart.

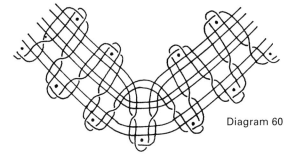

Diagram 60

Figure 22

When the heart shape is complete, make the diamond filling using weaver and inner passives.

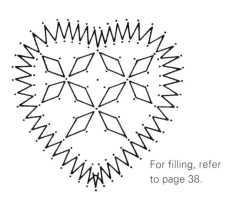

For filling, refer to page 38.

Pricking 22

Working direction

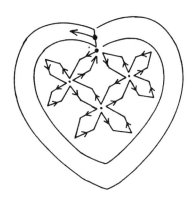

Diagram 59

23. Motif-4

Inner floral ring: 7 pairs. For diamond filling, use weaver and inner passives and make 4 diamond shapes.

Outer floral ring: 7 pairs. Join inner floral ring and outer one with plaits.

Working order
and direction

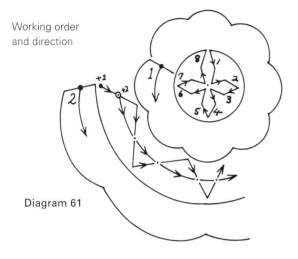

Diagram 61

Figure 23

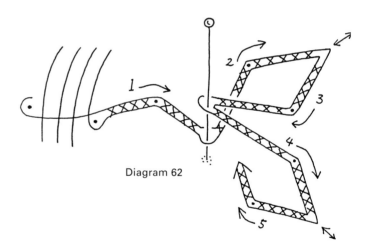

Diagram 62

Use crochet hook when 3 plaits have to be fastened off into one central pinhole.

Windmill crossing. Refer to page 134, diagram 234.

Pricking 23

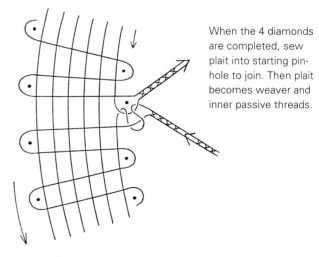

When the 4 diamonds are completed, sew plait into starting pinhole to join. Then plait becomes weaver and inner passive threads.

Diagram 63

24. Heart

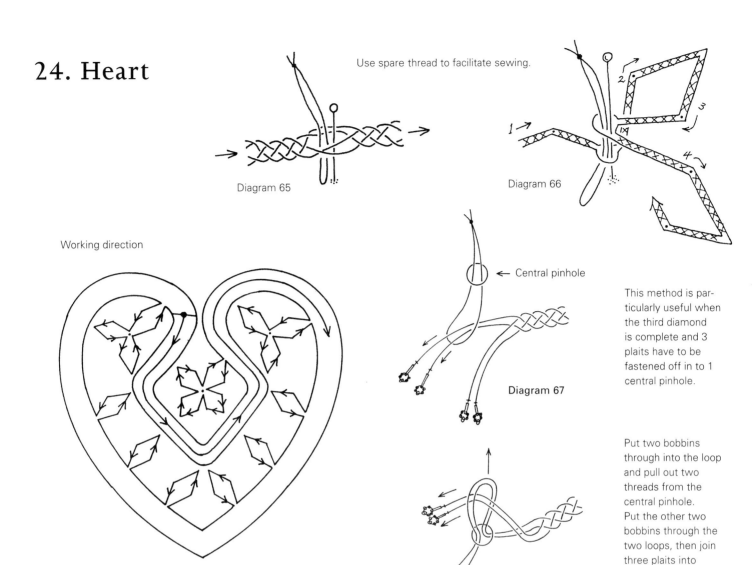

Use spare thread to facilitate sewing.

Diagram 65

Diagram 66

Working direction

Diagram 64

← Central pinhole

Diagram 67

This method is particularly useful when the third diamond is complete and 3 plaits have to be fastened off in to 1 central pinhole.

Diagram 68

Put two bobbins through into the loop and pull out two threads from the central pinhole. Put the other two bobbins through the two loops, then join three plaits into one. Remove the spare thread.

Pricking 24

Figure 24

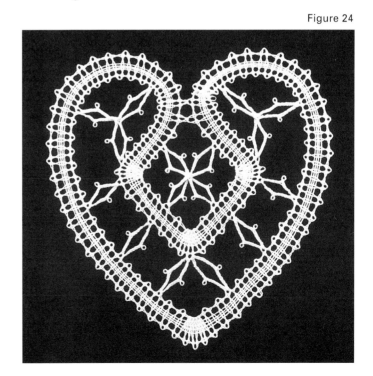

25. Flower-3

Flower and frame: 6 pairs.

Pricking 25

Working direction

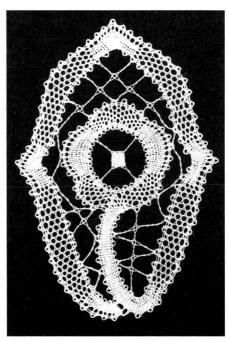

Diagram 69

Figure 25

26. Motif-5

Oval shape: 4 pairs.
Plaited edge: 4 pairs.
Start oval shape and plaited edge together, then work filling.

Figure 26

Pricking 26

Working direction

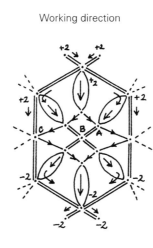

Diagram 70

27. Little Bird

Start whole-stitch braid with 3 pairs at the tail and continue to complete the body.

Second section: start from tip of wing with 3 pairs. Add twists on the weavers where shown in fig. 27.

Third section: neck band with 4 pairs worked in half-stitch with whole-stitch and twist before and after each pin.

Figure 27

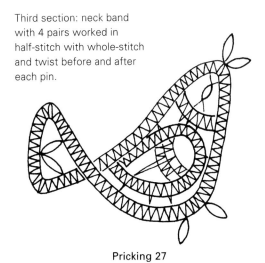

Pricking 27

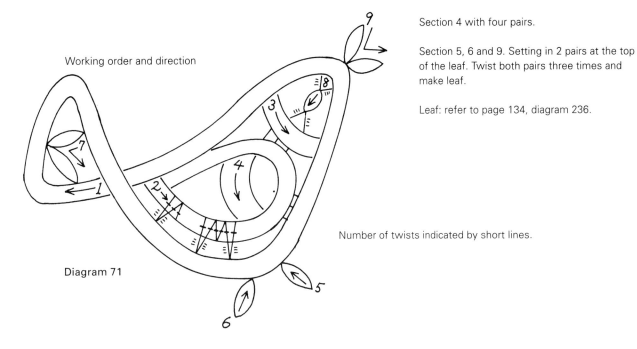

Working order and direction

Diagram 71

Section 4 with four pairs.

Section 5, 6 and 9. Setting in 2 pairs at the top of the leaf. Twist both pairs three times and make leaf.

Leaf: refer to page 134, diagram 236.

Number of twists indicated by short lines.

28. Snail

Guide to setting in and working the first section.

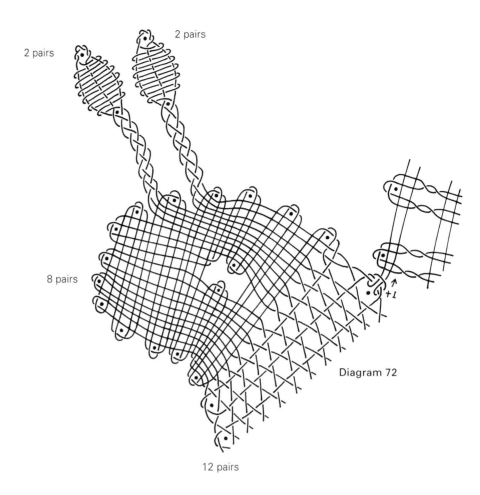

2 pairs

2 pairs

8 pairs

+1

Diagram 72

12 pairs

Decrease the pairs until 4 pairs are at the tip of the tail.
Decrease: refer to page 135, diagram 243.

Figure 28

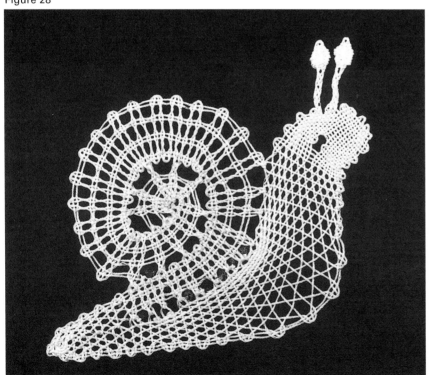

Make shell with 5 pairs. Commence in half-stitch, change to whole-stitch with twisted weavers where passive lines begin on pricking. Add 5th pair near head (see +1, diagram 72).

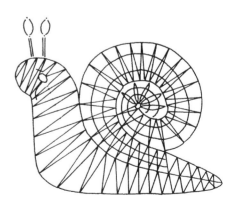

Pricking 28

29. Butterfly-3

Antenna: 4 pairs.
Head: add 2 pairs.
Total: 6 pairs.

Working
direction

Diagram 73

Figure 29

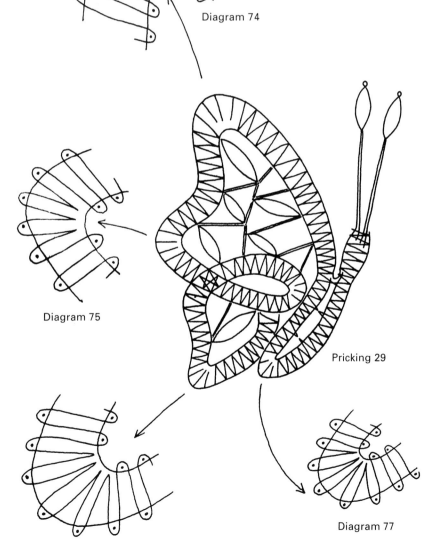

Diagram 74

Diagram 75

Diagram 76

Diagram 77

Pricking 29

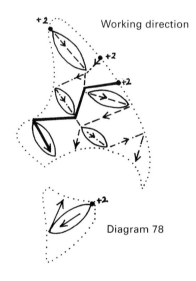

Working direction

+2
+2
+2
+2

Diagram 78

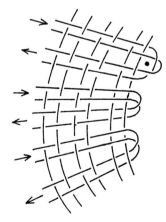

Method of
working inner
curves,
diagrams 74,
75, 76 and 77.

Diagram 79

43

30. Tropical Fish-2

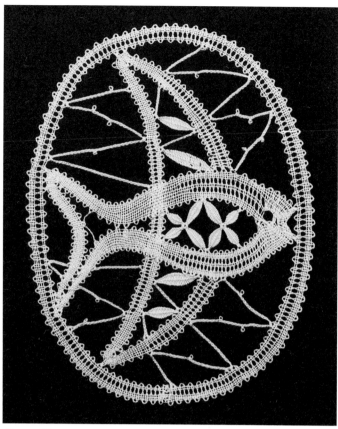

Figure 30

Start first section, oval shape, with four pairs.

Begin second section at the tip of tail with four pairs. Increase to six pairs to form body.

Working order and direction

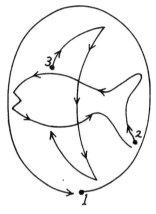

Diagram 80

Third section: a fin with 4 pairs.

Add twists on weavers as shown in figure 30.

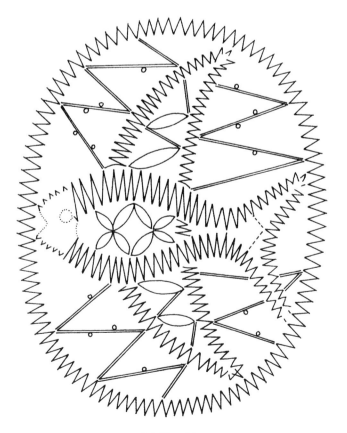

Pricking 30

Guide to working the head section.

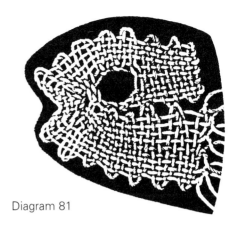

Diagram 81

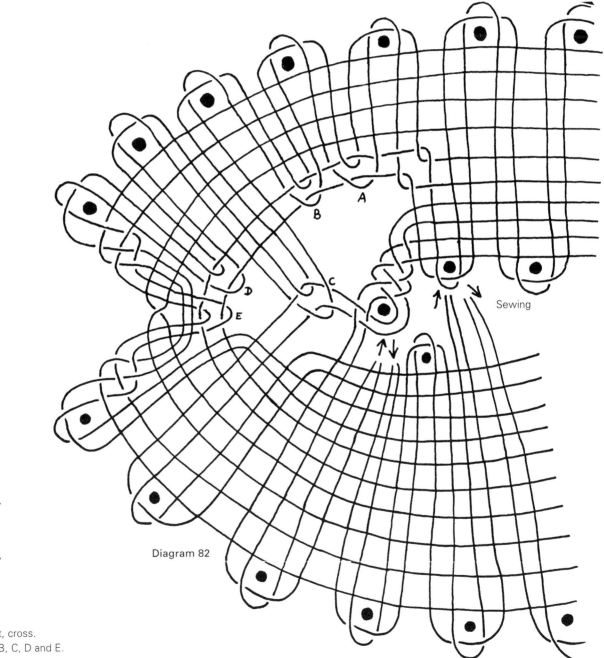

Sewing

Diagram 82

Diagram 83

Turning stitch:
Cross, twist, twist, cross.
Work these at A, B, C, D and E.

31. Mouse

Start the inner ring with four pairs plus 1 pair for centre. For the second section, body with three pairs, feet with three pairs.

Working order and direction

Diagram 84

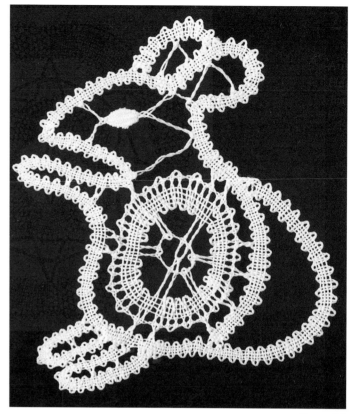

Figure 31

Guide to working eye and filling.

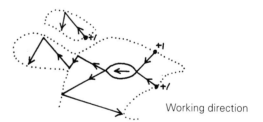

Working direction

Diagram 85

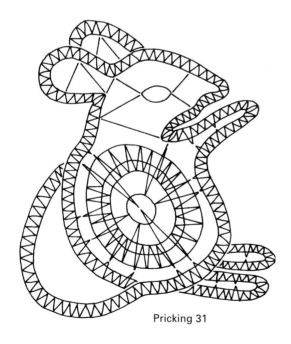

Pricking 31

32. Iris

Flower: 6 pairs.

Second section: 4 pairs.
Third section: 4 pairs.
Fourth section: 5 pairs.
Fifth section: 5 pairs.

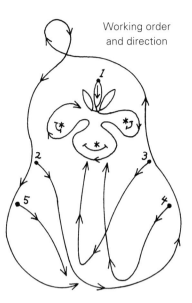

Working order
and direction

Diagram 86

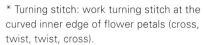

* Turning stitch: work turning stitch at the
curved inner edge of flower petals (cross,
twist, twist, cross).

Refer to page 45, diagram 83.

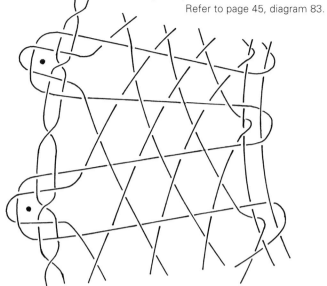

Diagram 87

Figure 32

Pricking 32

33. Butterfly-4

Start continuous trail with four pairs.

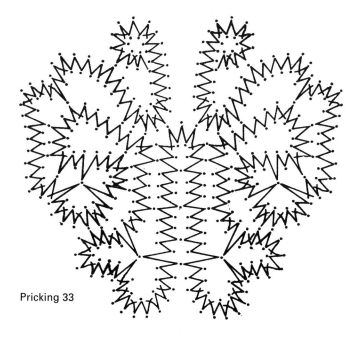

Pricking 33

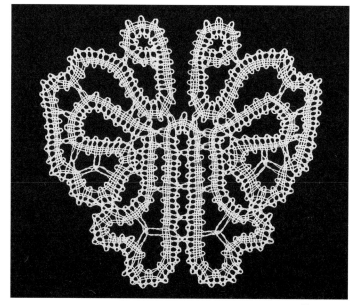

Figure 33

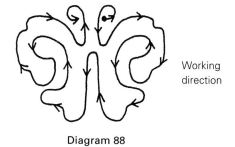

Working direction

Diagram 88

34. Tiny Star

4 pairs

Figure 34

Start

Pricking 34

35. Christmas tree-1

4 pairs

Decorate with beads and sequins.

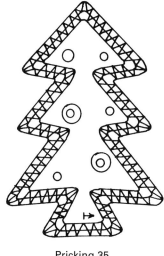

Pricking 35

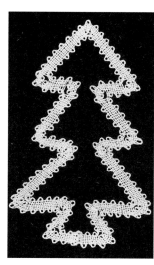

Figure 35

36. Christmas Star

Five pairs.

Guide to setting in and working the first section.

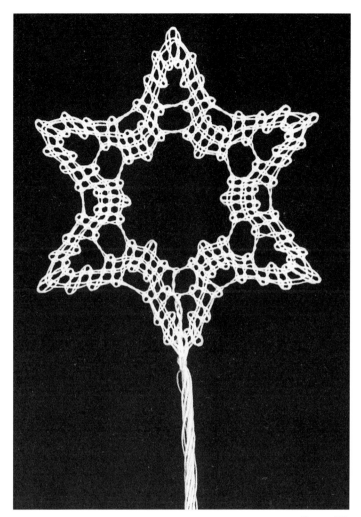

Figure 36

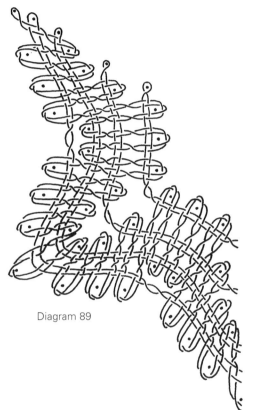

Diagram 89

Metallic gold and silver thread is ideal.

Suitable as an ornament for
Christmas trees and as a motif for
Christmas cards.

Finish off and bunch all
the threads into a tassel.

Pricking 36

37. Christmas Bell-1

Four pairs for
each section.

Working order

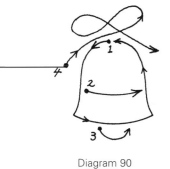

Diagram 90

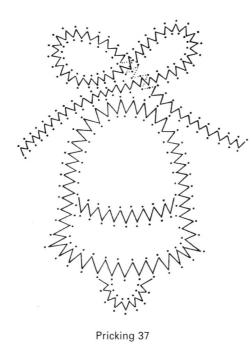

Pricking 37

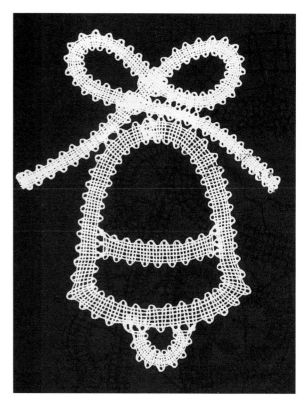

Figure 37

38. Star-3

Figure 38

Four pairs for
star shape.

Filling

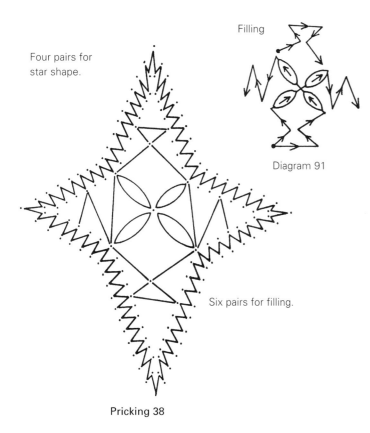

Six pairs for filling.

Pricking 38

Diagram 91

39. Cross

Guide to setting in and working the first section with 6 pairs.

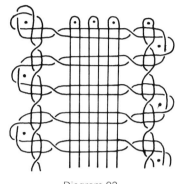

Diagram 92

Figure 39

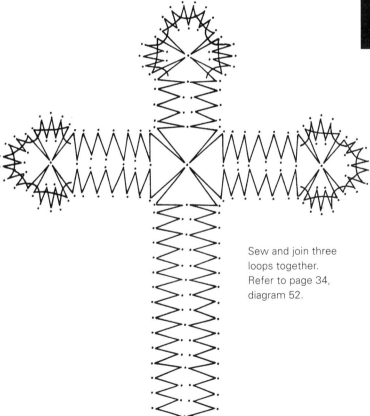

Sew and join three loops together. Refer to page 34, diagram 52.

Pricking 39

Working direction

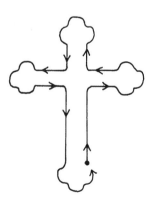

Diagram 93

40. Christmas Ornament

Work the first section with 4 pairs.
Section 2: 3 pairs.
Section 3: 7 pairs.
Section 4: 3 pairs.

Working order and direction

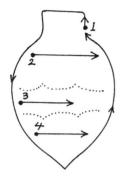

Diagram 94

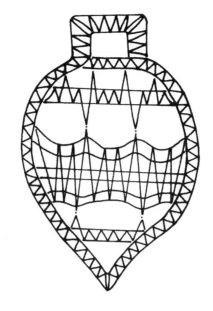

Pricking 40

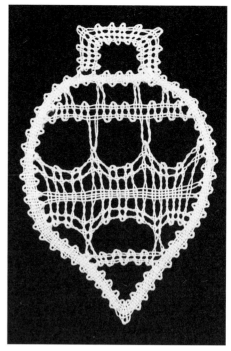

Figure 40

41. Stocking

Start with 2 pairs from the corner pinhole. When the plait loop is made, sew the plait into the first corner pinhole.

Change plait to weaver and passives. Add 2 extra pairs of passives and continue to make the outline of the stocking.

Figure 41

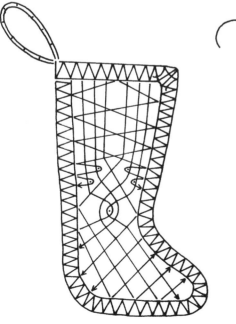

Pricking 41

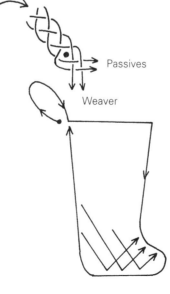

Diagram 95

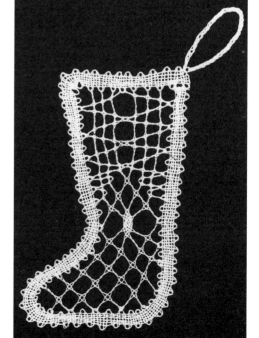

42. Christmas Bell-2

Section 1 and 2: 6 pairs.
Section 3 and 4: 4 pairs.

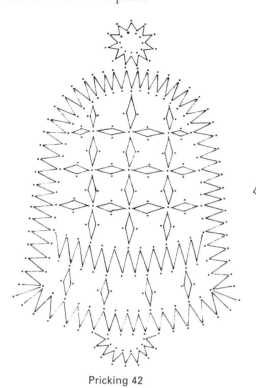

Pricking 42

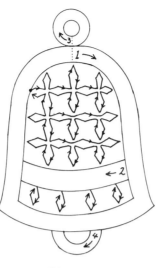

Diagram 96

Filling: refer to page 38.

Figure 42

43. Christmas Pudding

Work pudding with 3 pairs, plate with 6 pairs.
Filling is half-stitch, pin half-stitch.

Figure 43

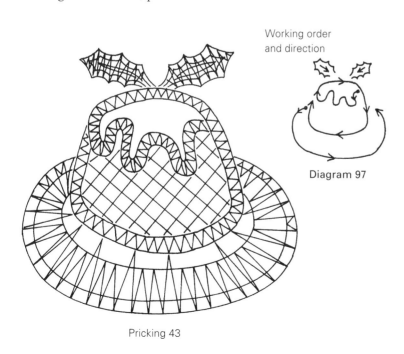

Pricking 43

Working order
and direction

Diagram 97

53

44. Candle

Start from the top of the flame
and continue to the candle.

Enlarged diagram for setting in
a new pair.

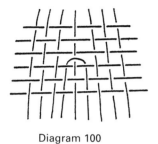

Diagram 100

Use threads from flame, adding
extra pairs as needed

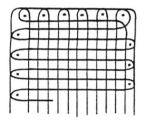

Diagram 101

Guide to setting
in and working
the first section

Diagram 98

'T' Setting in a pair

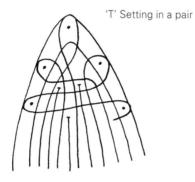

Diagram 99

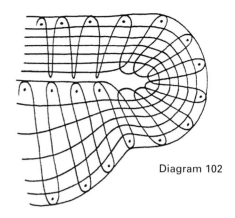

Diagram 102

Curve of handle

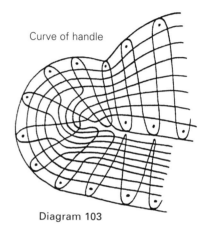

Diagram 103

Figure 44

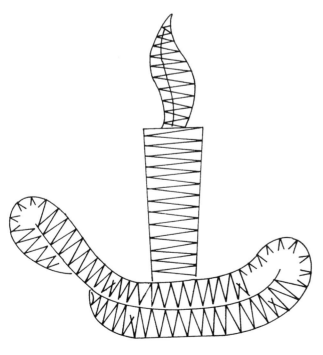

Pricking 44

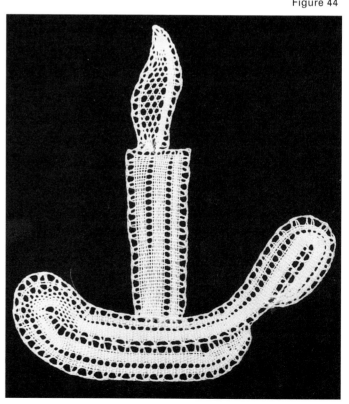

45. Christmas Tree - 2

Work the frame first then the Christmas tree.

When each diamond shape is complete, make the sewing and join to the starting pinhole. Refer to page 38, diagram 63.

Figure 45

Pricking 45

Diagram 104

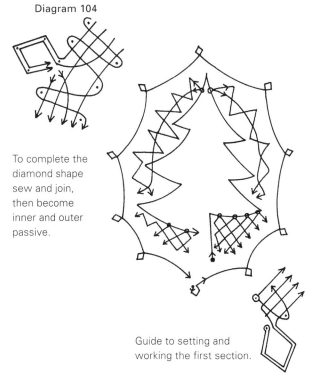

To complete the diamond shape sew and join, then become inner and outer passive.

Guide to setting and working the first section.

Diagram 105

46. Christmas Tree-3

Start from section one with 5 pairs.

Diagram 106

Section 3: Flame. When the flame is completed continue to make the candle.

Do not cut the threads; leave out 2 pairs for plait filling (5), use remaining pairs from the flame, plus centre flame pairs to make the candle.

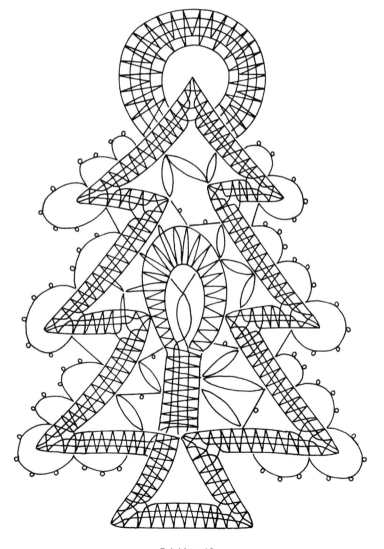

Pricking 46

Guide to setting and working
the first section.

5 pairs

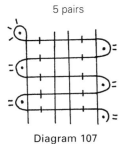

Diagram 107

Small dashes indicate number
of twists

Second section: 6 pairs.

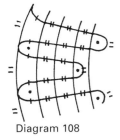

Diagram 108

Third section: 5 pairs.

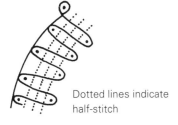

Dotted lines indicate
half-stitch

Diagram 109

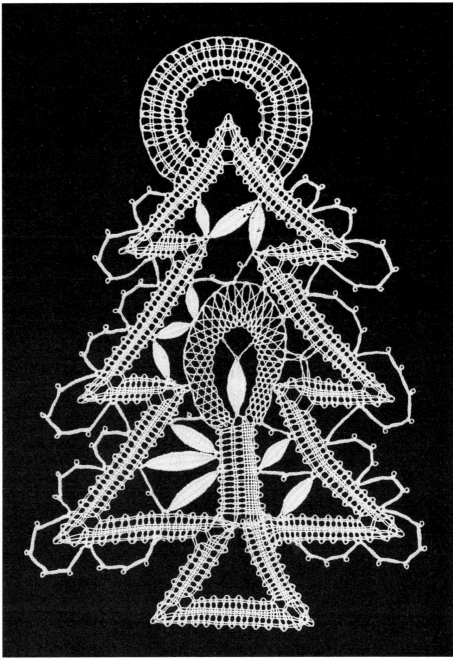

Figure 46

Angle of tree

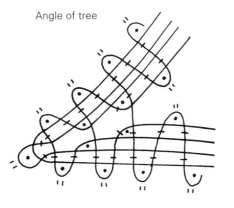

Pairs are indicated by
single lines.

Diagram 110

57

47. Christ

Start at the neck with 5 pairs.

Eyes and mouth

Standard picot and plait.

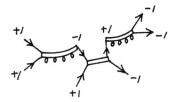

Diagram 111

Figure 47

Section 1: 5 pairs
Section 2: 6 pairs
Section 3: 5 pairs
Section 4: 5 pairs
Section 5: 4 pairs
Section 6: 2 pairs
Section 7: 4 pairs

Working order and direction

Diagram 112

Pricking 47

48. Angel

Work the face first then some passive threads can be used to continue to form the wings.

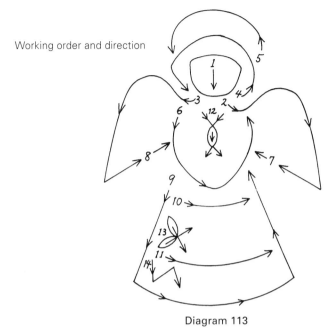

Working order and direction

Diagram 113

Figure 48

Pricking 48

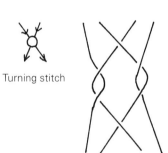

Turning stitch

Use turning stitches to form eyes and mouth.
Half-stitch, Twist, Half-stitch.

Diagram 114

Eyes and mouth

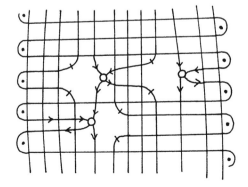

Diagram 115

49. Leaf

Set in 4 pairs at the top pin and make plaits on both sides.

Diagram 116

Guide to setting in and working the first section.

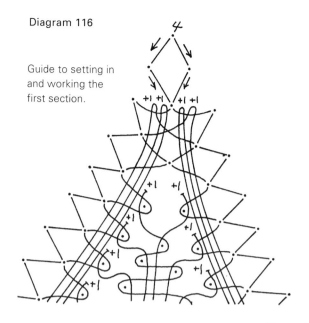

Figure 49

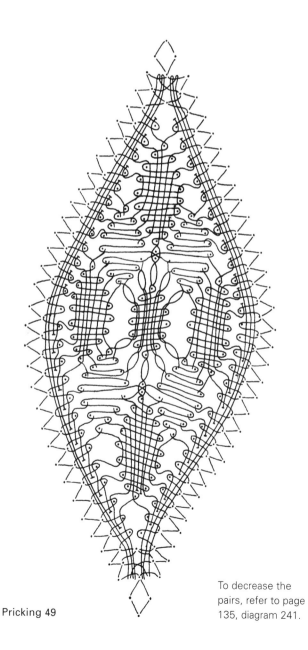

Pricking 49

To decrease the pairs, refer to page 135, diagram 241.

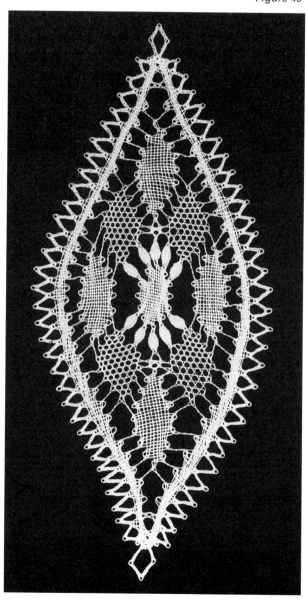

50. Aries - The Ram

21 March-19 April

Work the horn first with three pairs.

Tie and finish off.

Start the second section from the head with three pairs.

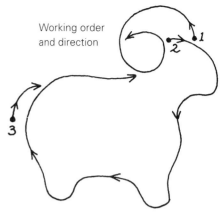

Working order and direction

Diagram 117

Third section: start from the tip of the tail with 3 pairs. Tie and finish off.

Set four pairs for filling. Refer to page 133, diagram 228.

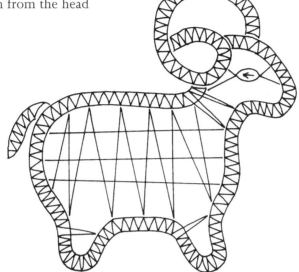

Pricking 50

Figure 50

51. Taurus - The Bull

20 April-20 May

Start from the horn with 3 pairs.

Second section. Head: 3 pairs.

Working order and direction

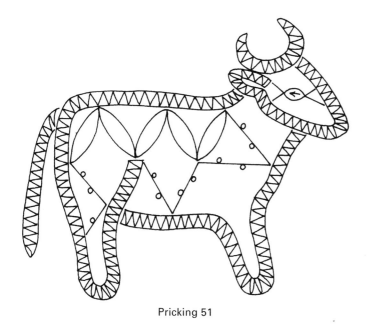

Diagram 118

Fourth Section: tail
with 3 pairs. Start
from the tip.

Refer to page 64,
diagram 121.

Pricking 51

Figure 51

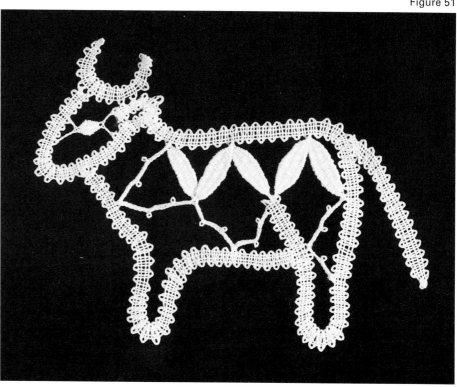

52. Gemini - The Twins

21 May-21 June

Start the hair section first with 3 pairs.

Working order and direction

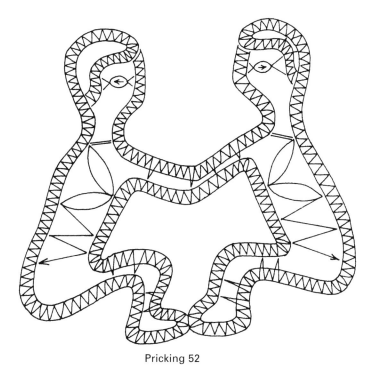

Pricking 52

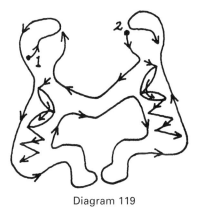

Diagram 119

For the second section, set in two pairs at a pin for a weaver and passives.

Set in one pair at a neighbouring pin. Refer to page 133.

Figure 52

53. Cancer - The Crab

22 June-22 July

Start from the base of the shell with three pairs.

To form the eyes use weaver and outer passive pairs and make a plait. Refer to the eye diagram 131 on page 69.

Working order and direction

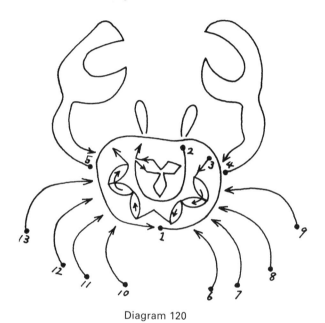

Diagram 120

Guide to setting in and working each leg.

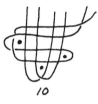

Diagram 121

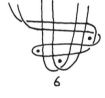

Diagram 122

Pricking 53

Figure 53

54. Leo - The Lion

23 July-22 August

Start from the mane with three pairs, then make the tail. Start from the tip with 3 pairs.

Working order and direction

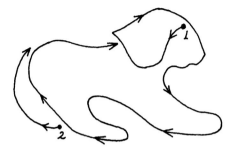

Diagram 123

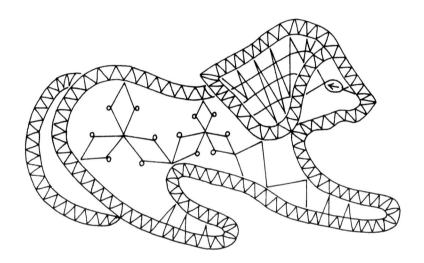

Pricking 54

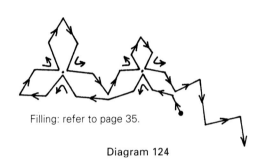

Filling: refer to page 35.

Diagram 124

Figure 54

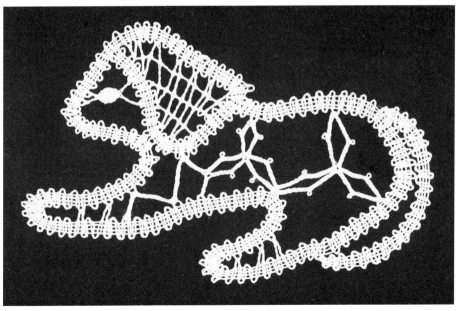

55. Virgo - The Virgin

23 August-22 September

Start at the shoulder with three pairs.

For the hair section use three pairs.

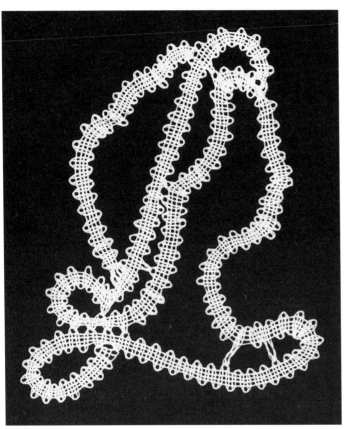

Figure 55

Working order and direction

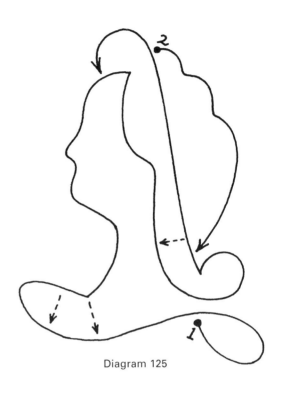

Diagram 125

Guide to showing
twisted weaver and
sewing

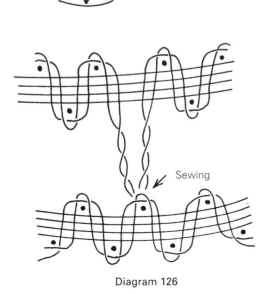

Sewing

Diagram 126

Pricking 55

56. Libra - The Scales

23 September-23 October

When the fifth section is complete,
make a plait using 2 pairs for section 6.
Continue in the same manner for
sections 7 and 8.

Working order and direction

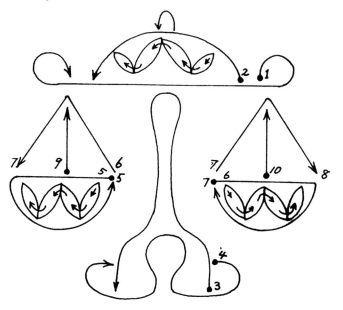

Diagram 127

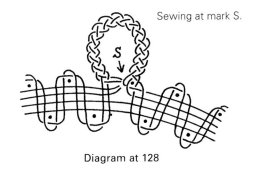

Sewing at mark S.

Diagram at 128

Pricking 56

67

57. Scorpio - The Scorpion

24 October-21 November

Start at head using 6 pairs.

From the centre, work to both sides in whole-stitch.

To make the eyes use weaver and outer passives, making a plait to form the eye.

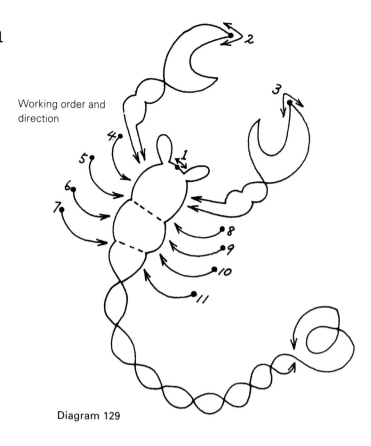

Working order and direction

Diagram 129

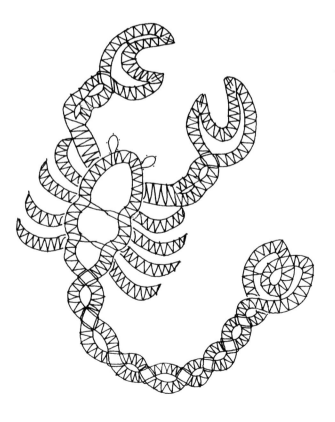

Pricking 57

Figure 57

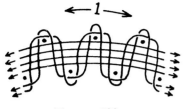

Diagram 130

Cross and change weavers of the body.

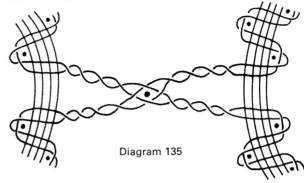

Diagram 135

Eye

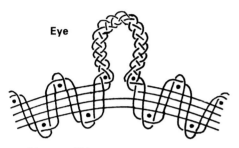

Diagram 131

Guide to showing working of the tail.

Sewing at mark S

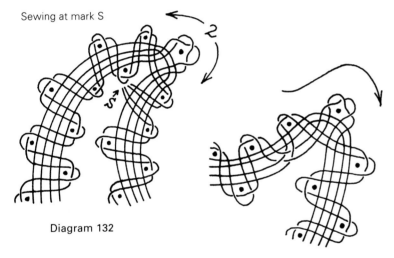

Diagram 132

Diagram 133

Diagram 136

Start at section 5

Diagram 134

Start at section 9

Diagram 138

Start at section 8

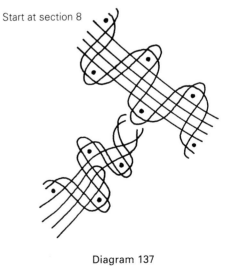

Diagram 137

58. Sagittarius - The Archer

22 November-21 December

Start at the arrow with 2 pairs.

Figure 58

Working order and direction

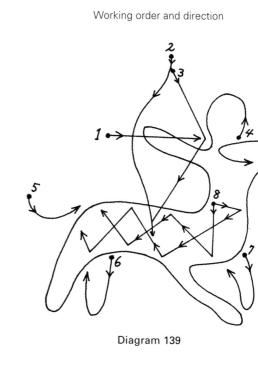

Diagram 139

Guide to setting in and working the
first section of the bow and string.

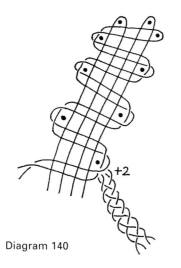

Diagram 140

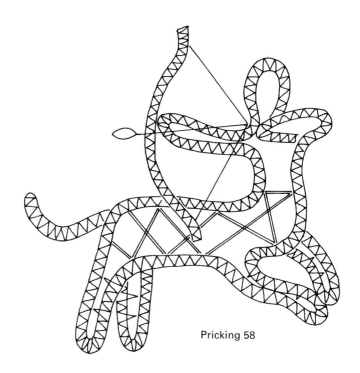

Pricking 58

59. Capricorn - The Goat

22 December-19 January

Start at the ear with 3 pairs, then form the head and horn.

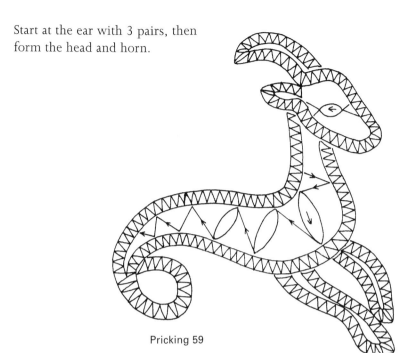

Pricking 59

Working order and direction

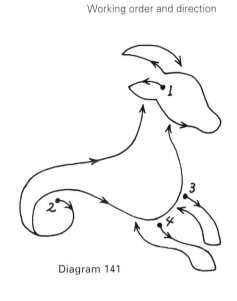

Diagram 141

Figure 59

For the second section start at the tip of the tail with 3 pairs.

Add 2 more pairs as passives and divide the passive threads into 2 parts.

Add the other weaver and continue to make two whole-stitch braids separately.

60. Aquarius - The Water Carrier

20 January - 18 February

Start at the face with 3 pairs.

Set in 3 pairs for the second section. Refer to page 133, diagram 228. Set in 1 pair in one pinhole and set in 2 pairs at second pinhole. Refer to page 133, diagram 229.

In the second section take weaver, twist several times and sew at the pinhole of the previously made trail. Twist several times and continue to work. For twist and sewing refer to page 66, diagram 126.

Working order and direction

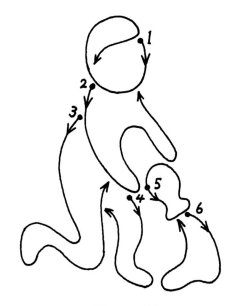

Diagram 142

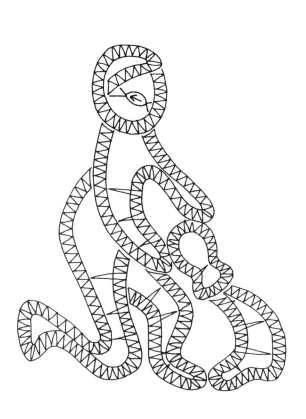

Pricking 60

Figure 60

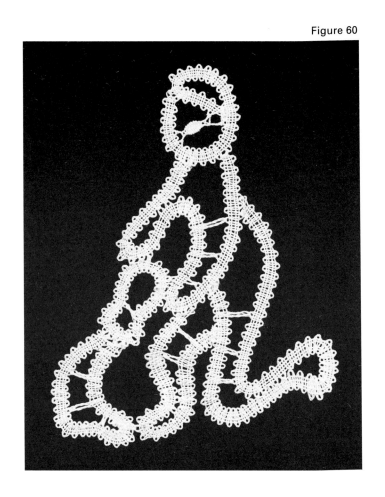

61. Pisces - The Fishes

19 February-20 March

Start at the mouth of the upper fish and continue to the lower fish using 3 pairs. Tie and finish. Work the gills with 3 pairs. Make the eyes and filling.

Working direction

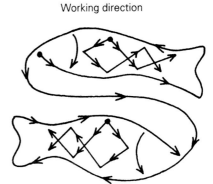

Diagram 143

Pricking 61

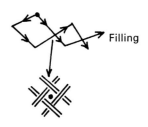

Filling

Diagram 144

Windmill crossing
Refer to page 134, diagram 234.

Figure 61

62. Spring

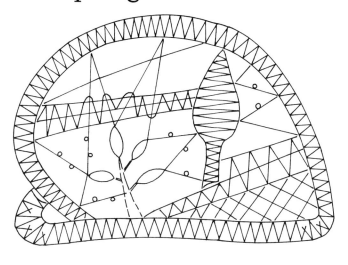

Pricking 62

Figure 62

For Spring motif
Make outer edge with 5 pairs first,
then the ground and trees, followed
by the sky.

63. Summer

For the Summer motif
Make the outer oval edge with 5
pairs.
Second section: yacht.
Third section: wave and sea.
Fourth section: sun.

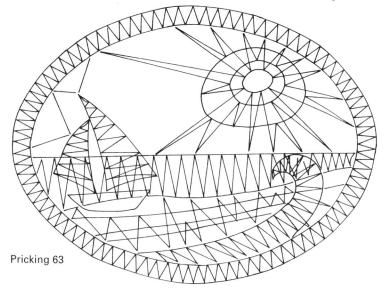

Pricking 63

Figure 63

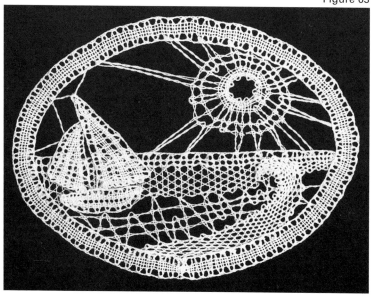

64. Autumn

Make the rectangular
frame first with 6 pairs.
Second section: tree.
Third section: field.
Fourth section: leaves

Pricking 64

Figure 64

65. Winter

Figure 65

Make the oval frame first
with 4 pairs.

Second section: centre
tree. Start from the base
of trunk.

Third section: side trees.
Start from the bases.

Fourth section: sun and
filling

Pricking 65

66. Tropical Fish-3

Start at the first section with four pairs.

Guide to showing the crossing over at mark a (sewing at four corners).

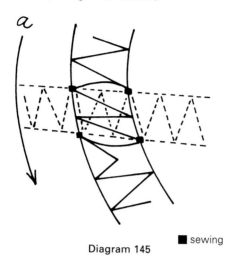

Guide to showing the crossing over at mark b.

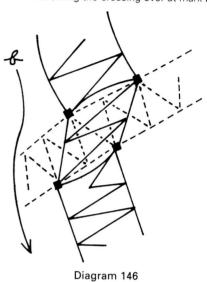

■ sewing

Diagram 145

Diagram 146

Pricking 66

Working order and direction

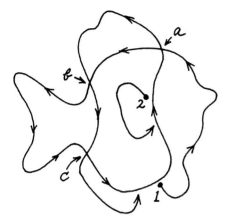

Diagram 147

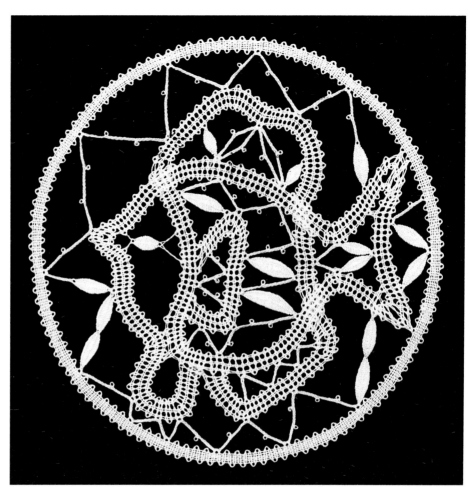

Figure 66

Guide to working crossing over at
mark c. Sewing at four corners.

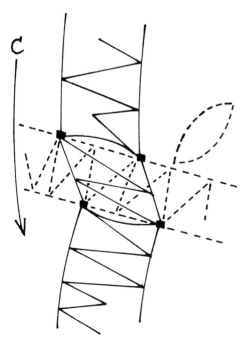

Diagram 148

67. Turtle

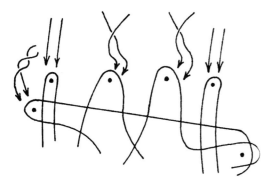

Guide to setting in and finishing of section 2, the outer edge of the shell.

Diagram 149

Diagram 150

Guide to setting in and finishing section 1,
inner ring of shell.

Sew weaver a, b to pinhole A.
Sew outer passives c, d to pinhole B.
Using these two pairs make leaves between
the inner ring and the outer edge of the shell.

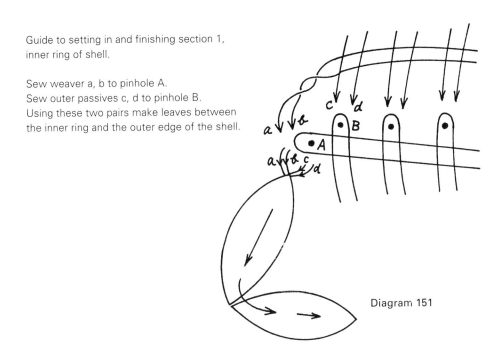

Diagram 151

Figure 67

Tail

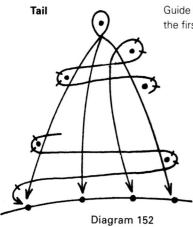

Guide to setting in and working
the first section with 3 pairs.

Diagram 152

Head

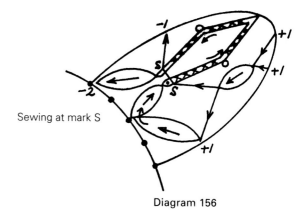

Sewing at mark S

Diagram 156

Starting the tail

Diagram 153

Diagram 154

Diagram 155

Pricking 67

68. Mushroom

Start the first section with 6 Pairs

Diamond filling. Refer page 38

Windmill crossing. Refer to page 134, diagram 234.

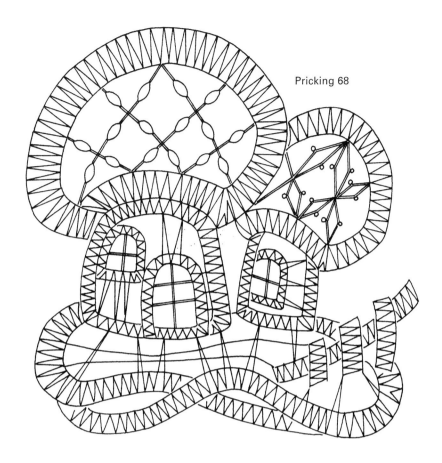

Pricking 68

Figure 68

Working order and direction

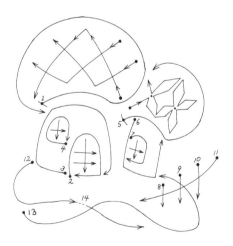

Diagram 157

69. Clown

Working order and direction

Nose and mouth

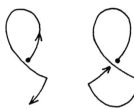

Diagram 158

Eyes

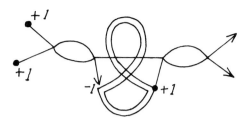

Diagram 159

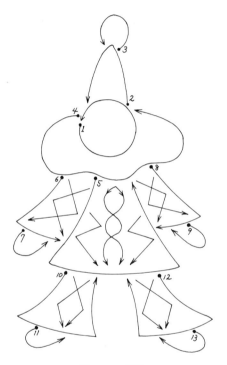

Diagram 160

Pricking 69

Number of bobbins
for each section:

Section 1: 3 pairs.
Section 2: 5 pairs.
Section 4: 5 pairs.
Section 5: 5 pairs.
Section 6: 5 pairs.
Section 7: 4 pairs.
Section 8: 5 pairs.
Section 9: 4 pairs.
Section 10: 5 pairs.
Section 11: 4 pairs.
Section 12: 5 pairs.
Section 13: 4 pairs.

Guide to showing how to turn
the corner of sleeve

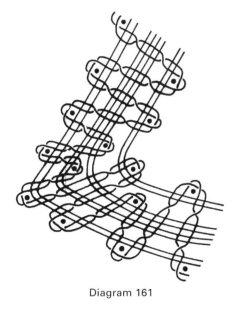

Diagram 161

Figure 69

70. Fish

Start at gill with 5 pairs.

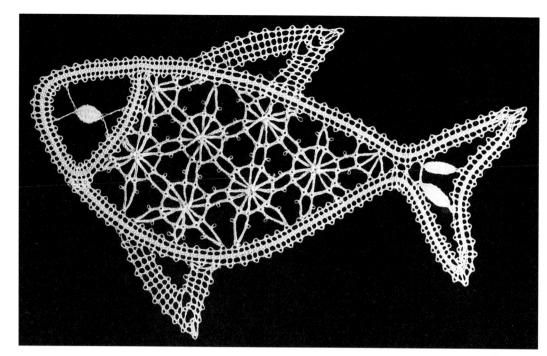

Figure 70

Knotted picot
Refer to page 135

Diagram 162

Windmill crossing.
Refer to page 134.

Diagram 163

Sewing
Refer to page 134

Diagram 164

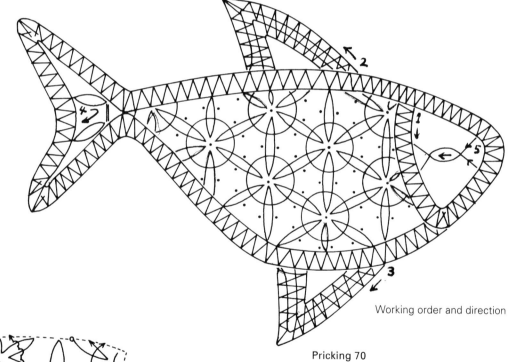

Working order and direction

Pricking 70

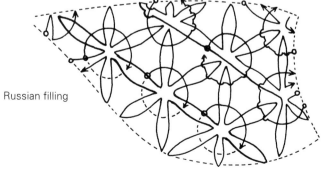

Russian filling

Diagram 165

71. Flower-4

Work flower petal with 5 pairs.

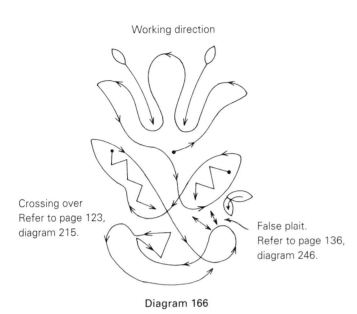

Working direction

Crossing over
Refer to page 123,
diagram 215.

False plait.
Refer to page 136,
diagram 246.

Diagram 166

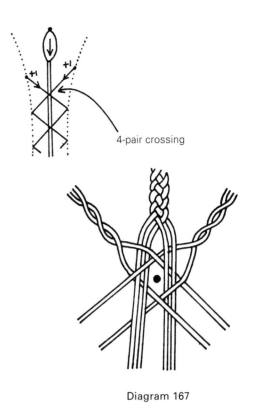

4-pair crossing

Diagram 167

Figure 71

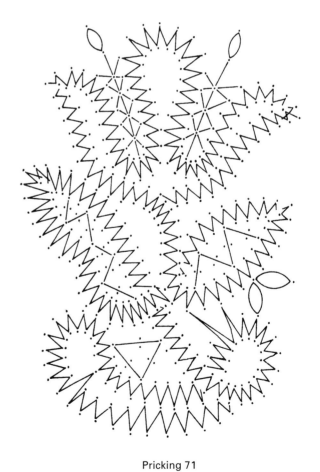

Pricking 71

72. Flower-5

Start from the centre ring of flower with 7 pairs
and continue to the stem and then the leaves.

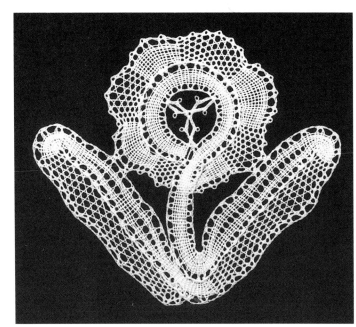

Figure 72

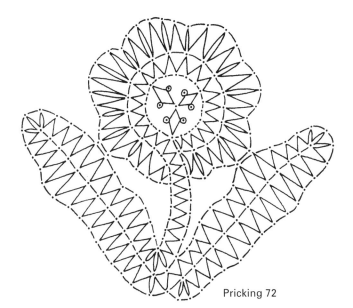

Pricking 72

Work raised sewings when joining outer
petals to centre ring. Refer to page 136,
diagram 247.

Pricking for wedding bell

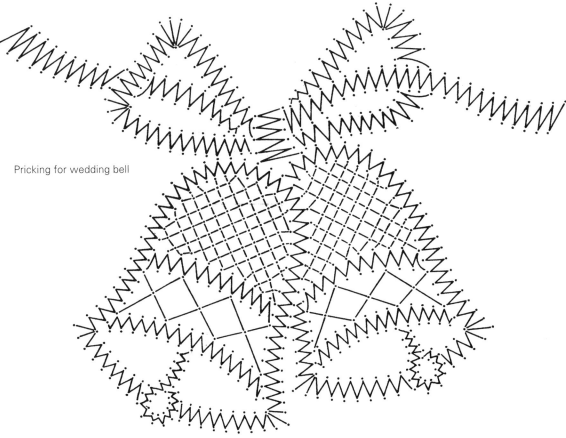

Pricking 73

73. Wedding Bell

Start the first section with 5 pairs.

Working order and direction

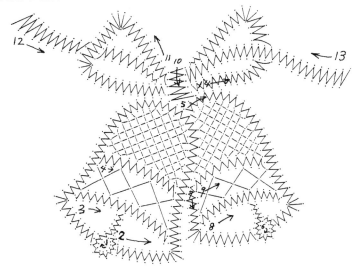

Diagram 168

Figure 73

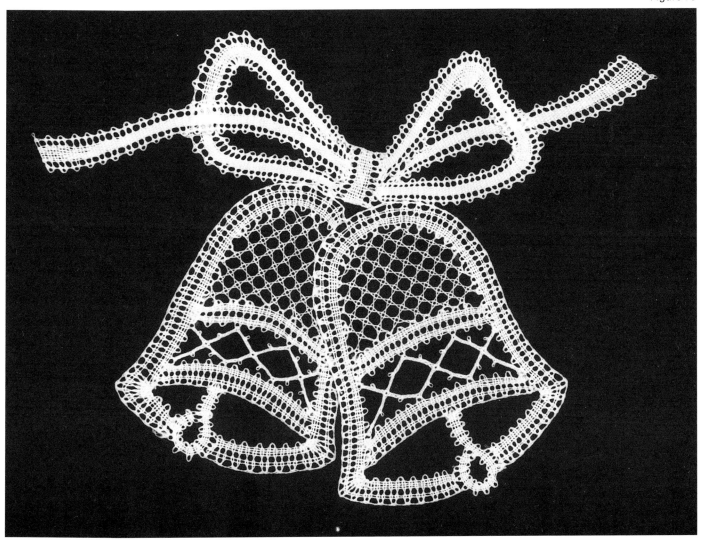

74. Flower Basket

Start from central flower with 5 pairs

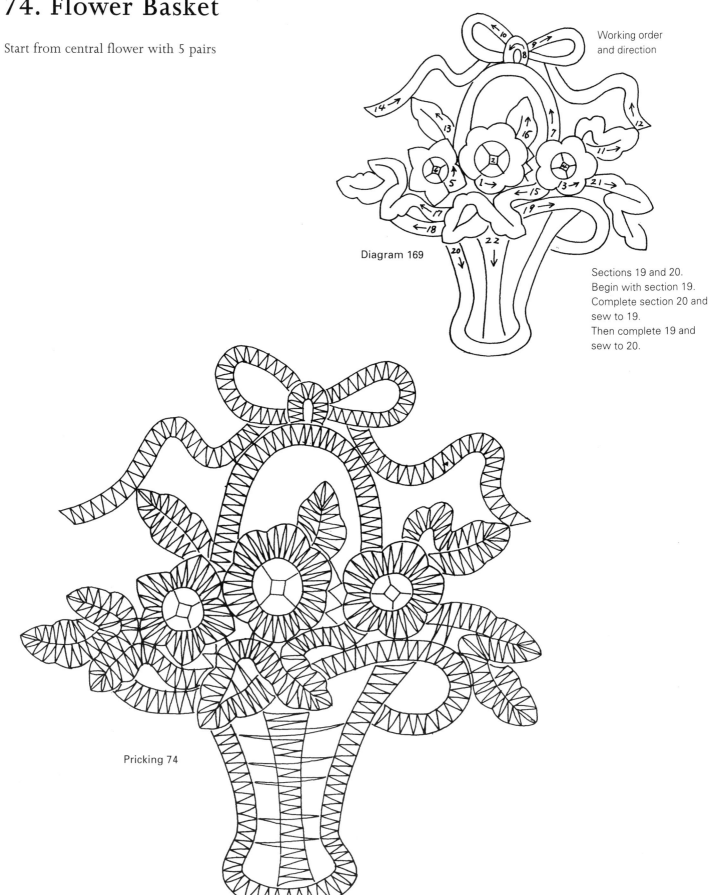

Working order and direction

Diagram 169

Sections 19 and 20.
Begin with section 19.
Complete section 20 and
sew to 19.
Then complete 19 and
sew to 20.

Pricking 74

Figure 74

75. Singing Birds

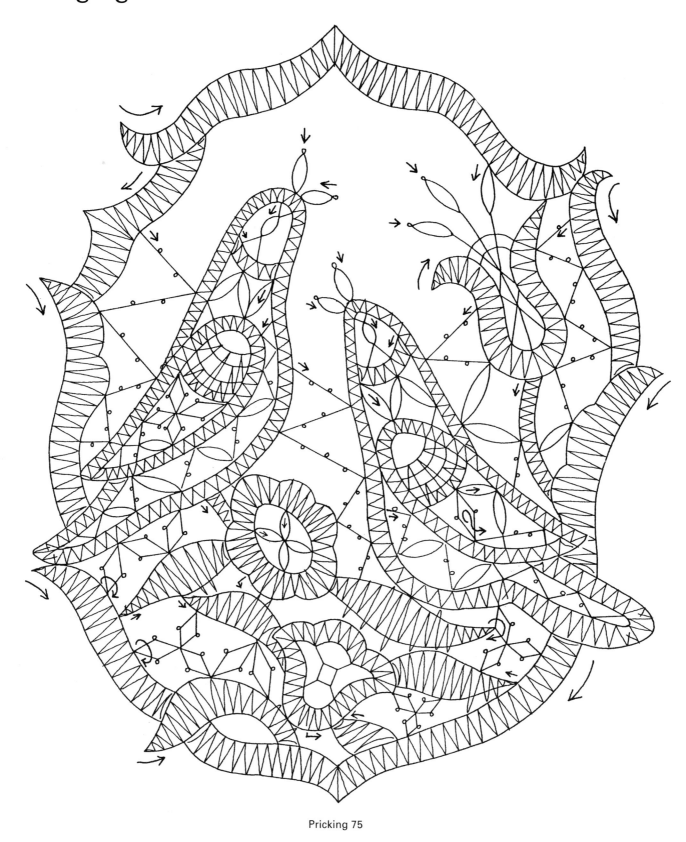

Pricking 75

Figure 75

Working order and direction

Start the first section, the tip of the wing, with 3 pairs.

Diagram 170

76. Young Girl

Figure 76

Working order and direction

Start from the face and continue to the bodice and skirt.

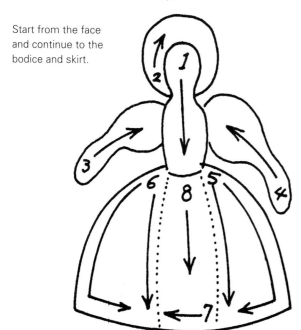

Diagram 171

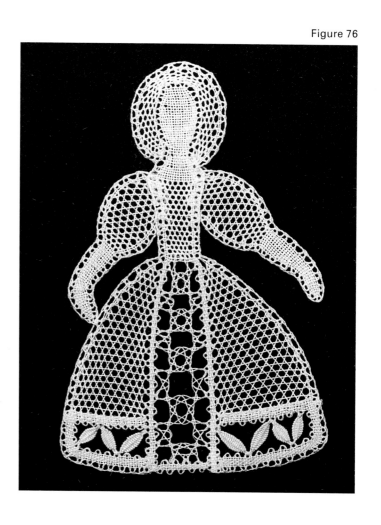

77. Silhouette

Start the first section with 5 pairs.

Working order and direction

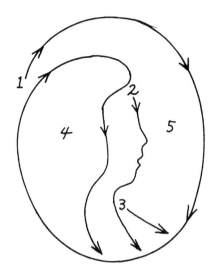

Diagram 172

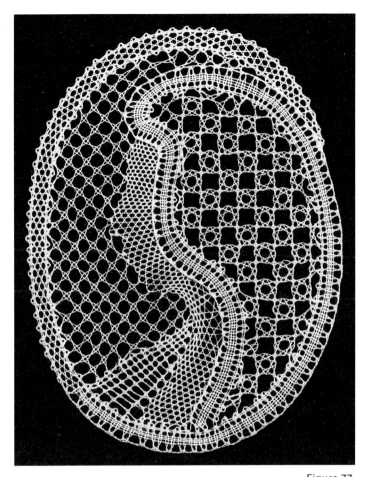

Figure 77

Pricking of young girl

Pricking 76

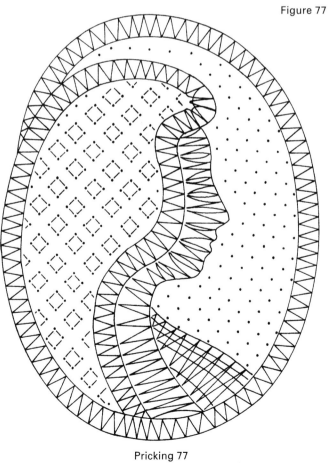

Pricking 77

93

78. Victorian Young Lady

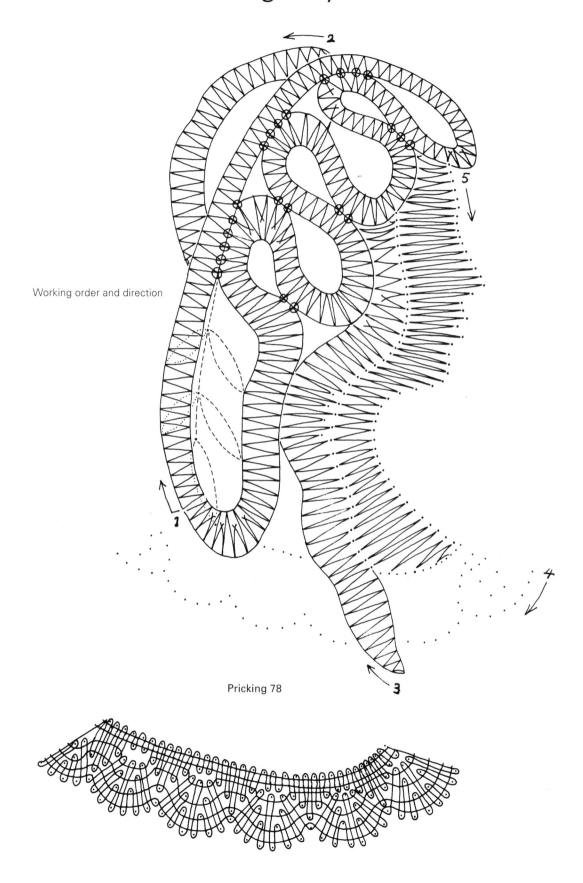

Working order and direction

Pricking 78

Figure 78

79. Victorian Lady

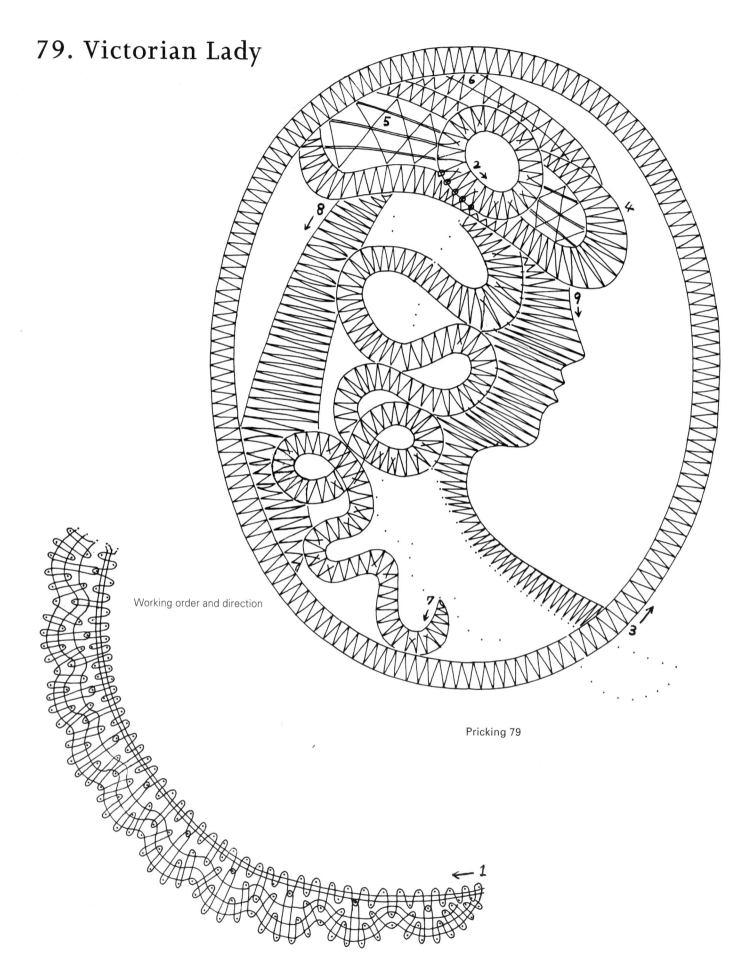

Working order and direction

Pricking 79

Figure 79

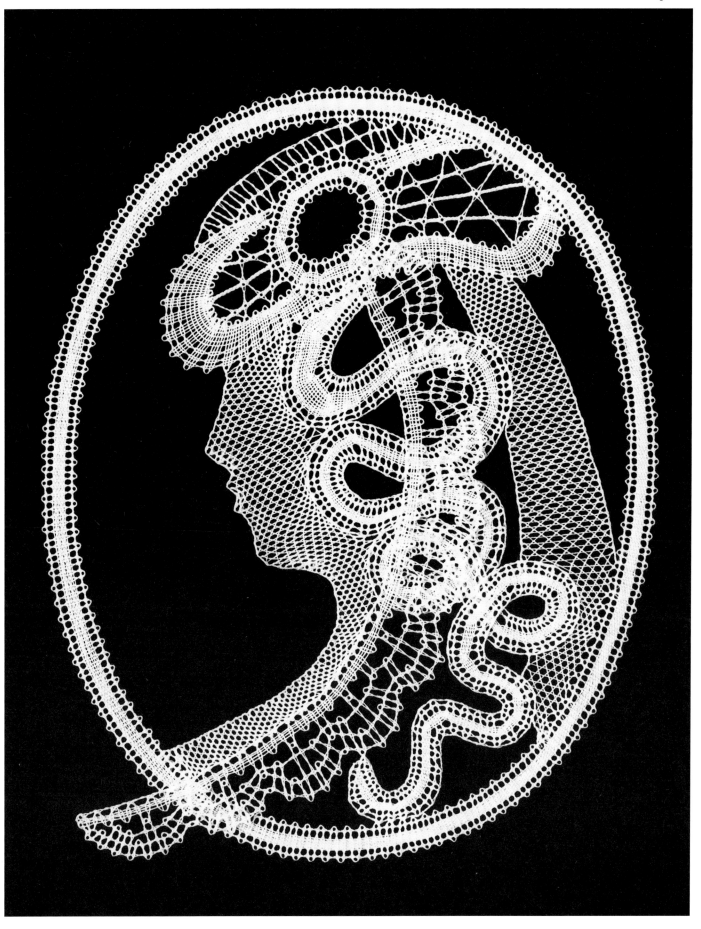

80. Swan Lake (Odette)

Figure 80

81. Swan Lake (Siegfried)

Figure 81

Working order and direction

Diagram 173

Pricking 81

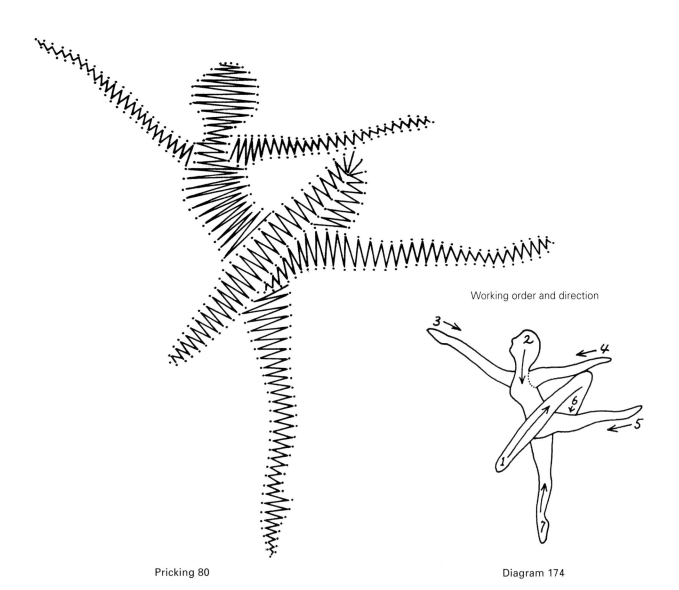

Working order and direction

Pricking 80   Diagram 174

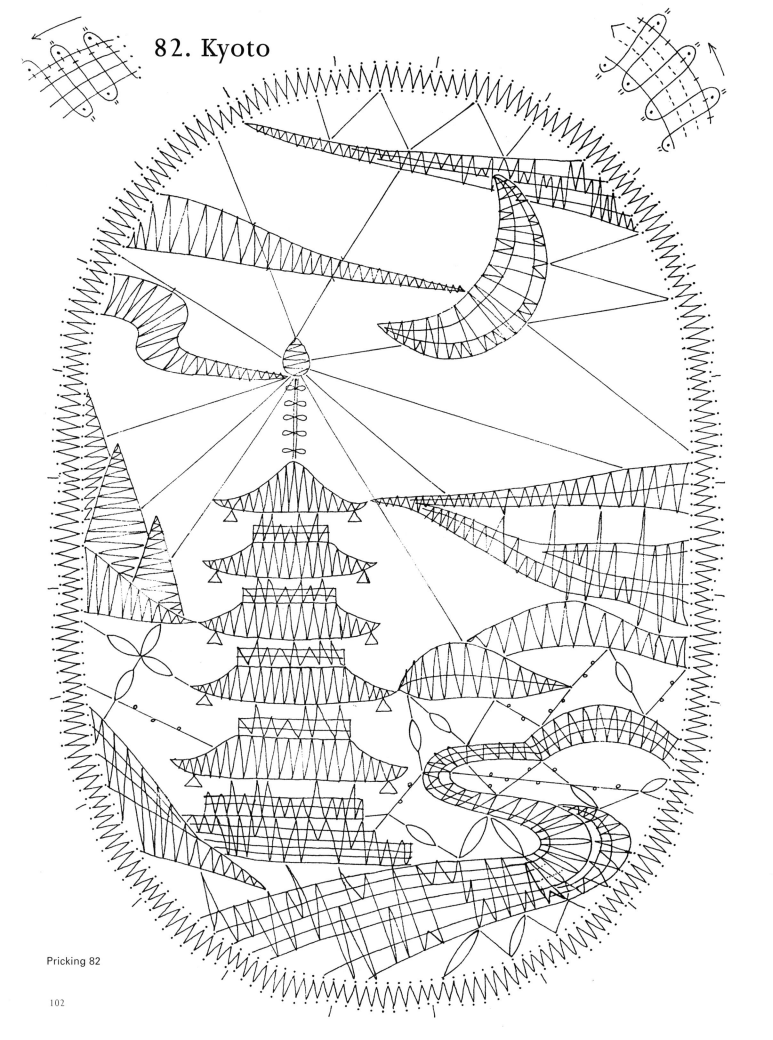

82. Kyoto

Figure 82

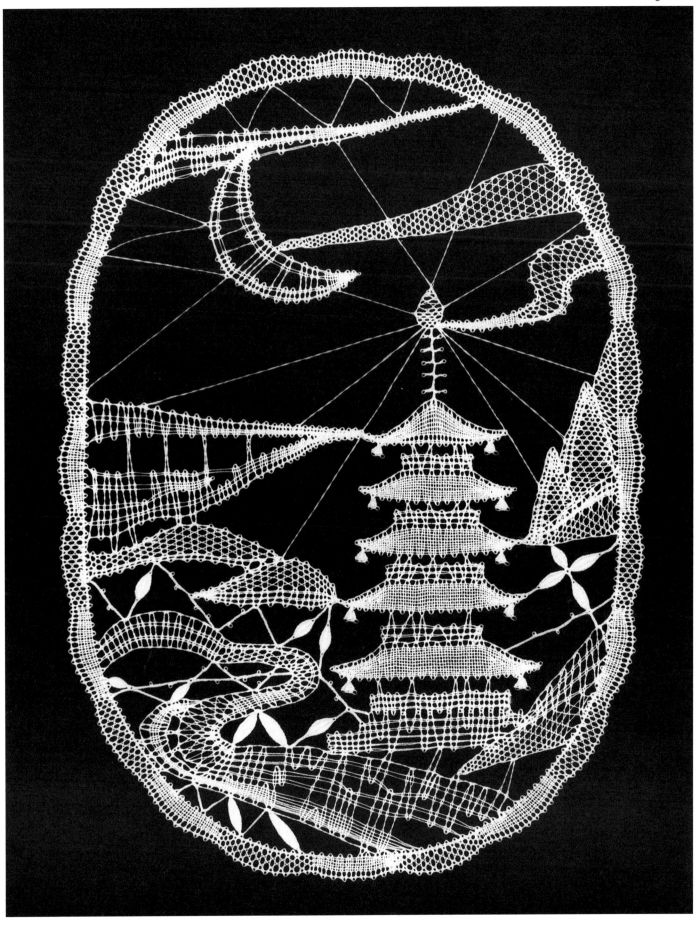

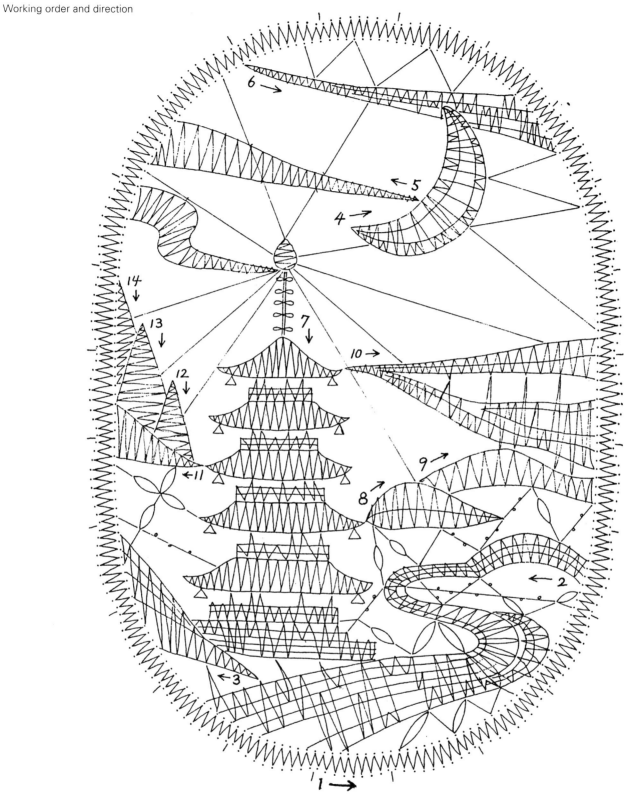

Diagram 175

Bell of roof

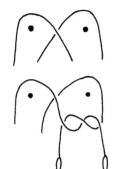

Diagram 176

Diagram 177

Setting in

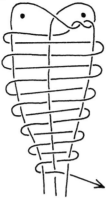

Diagram 178

Finishing bell

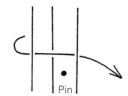

Diagram 179

Diagram 180

Diagram 181

83. Motif-6

7 pairs

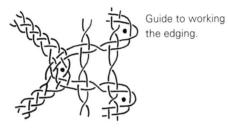

Guide to working
the edging.

Diagram 182

Figure 83

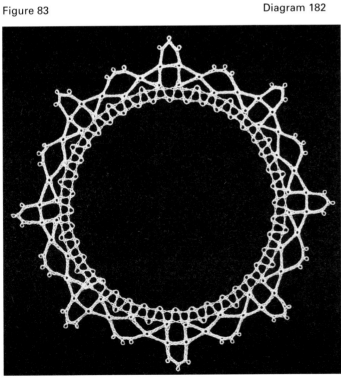

Pricking 83

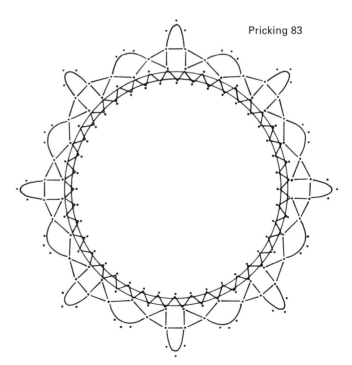

84. Motif-7

14 pairs.

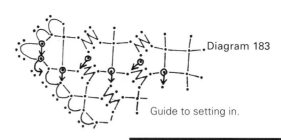

Diagram 183

Guide to setting in.

Pricking 84

Figure 84

85. Motif-8

13 pairs.
4 pairs for filling.

Guide to working the filling.

Diagram 184

Figure 85

Pricking 85

86. Motif-9

Section 1: 6 pairs.
Section 2: 4 pairs.

Working order and direction

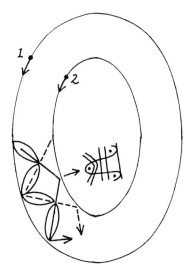

Diagram 185

Crossing with plait and
leaf. Refer to page 26,
diagram 31.

Figure 86

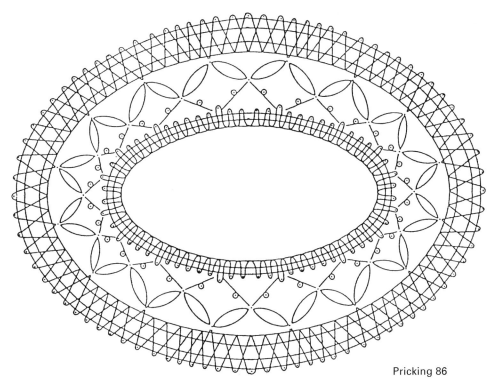

Pricking 86

87. Motif-10

Flower: 8 pairs.
Braid: 8 pairs.
Edging: 4 pairs.

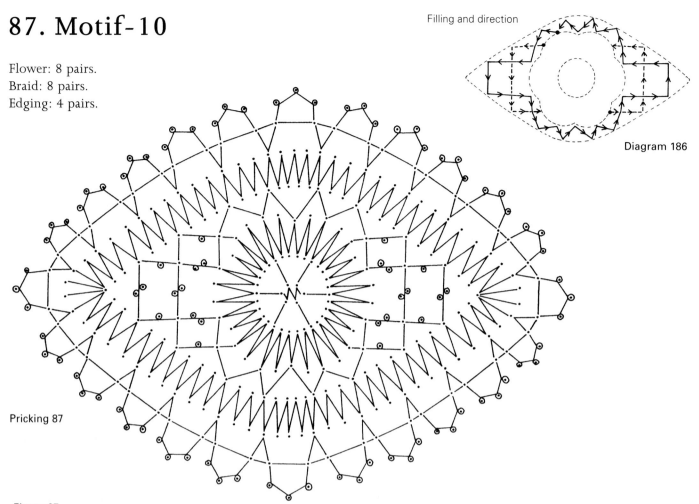

Diagram 186

Pricking 87

Figure 87

88. Floral Motif

Section 1: 7 pairs.
See diagram 187.
Section 2: 5 pairs.
Section 3: 7 pairs.

Filling
Centre of flower
refer to page 38.

Figure 88

Pricking 88

Working order and direction

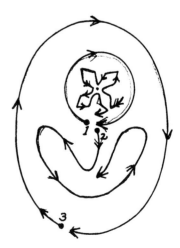

Diagram 187

89. Motif-11

Continuous braid with 8 pairs.

Windmill crossing

Diagram 189

Half-stitch
block (or circle)

Diagram 188

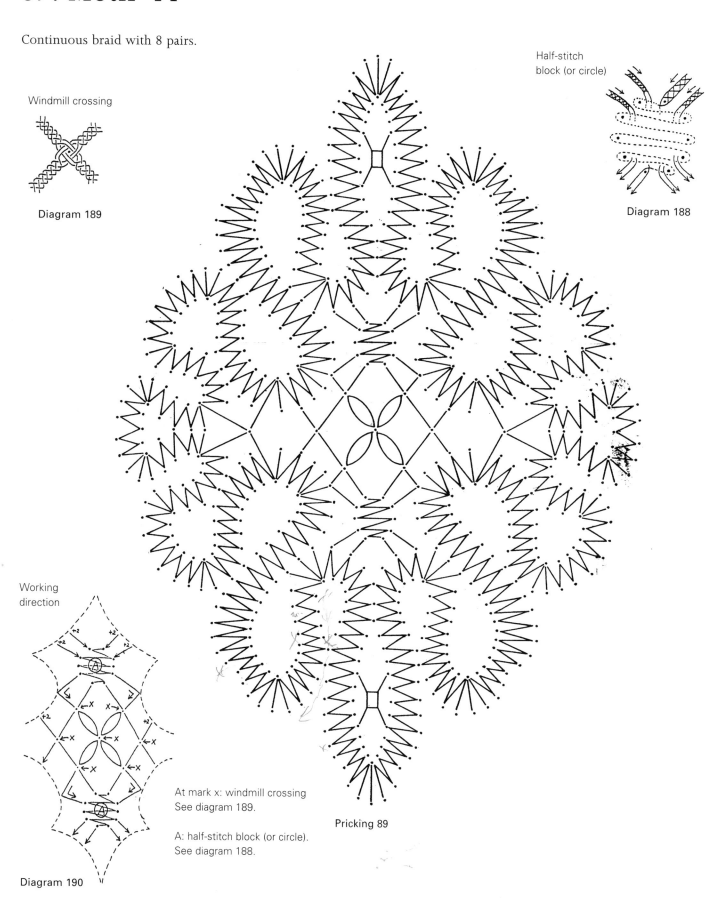

Working
direction

Diagram 190

At mark x: windmill crossing
See diagram 189.

A: half-stitch block (or circle).
See diagram 188.

Pricking 89

Figure 89

90. Motif-12

Continuous braid with 6 pairs.

Working order
and direction

Pricking 90

Filling

+ 4

Diagram 192

Diagram 191

Figure 90

91. Motif-13

Central flower: 8 pairs.
Inner trail: 7 pairs.
Outer edge: 8 pairs.

Working order and direction

Centre filling

Diagram 194

Diagram 193

Refer to page 38,
diagram 63.

Pricking 91

Sewing

Sewing

Diagram 195

Diagram 196

Figure 91

92. Motif-14

Central flower: 7 pairs.
Inner trail: 7 pairs.
Outer edge: 7 pairs.

Working order and direction

Diagram 197

Filling

Pricking 92

Filling

Diagram 198

Diagram 199

Figure 92

93. Handkerchief Corner-1

Working order and direction

Diagram 200

Section 1: 6 pairs.
Section 2: 6 pairs.
Section 3: 2 pairs.
Section 4: 2 pairs.

Figure 93

Diagram 201

Diagram 202

Diagram 203

Sewing

Sewing

Filling eyelets

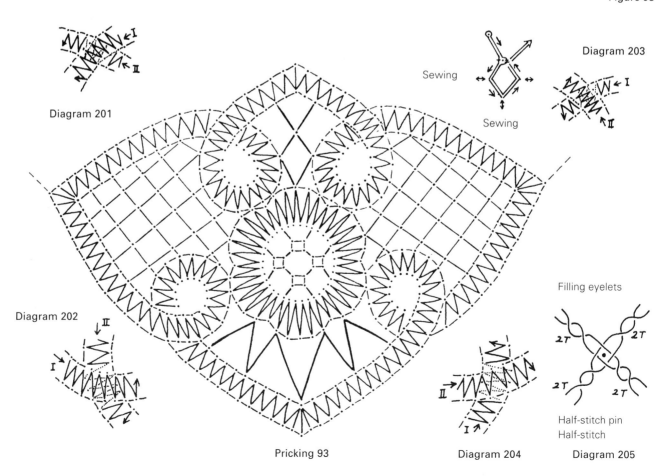

Pricking 93

Diagram 204

Half-stitch pin
Half-stitch

Diagram 205

94. Handkerchief Corner-2

Continuous trail with 6 pairs.
Plaited edging with 4 pairs.
False plait. Refer to page 136,
diagram 246.

Figure 94

Working direction

Diagram 206

Pricking 94

95. Handkerchief Corner-3

Section 1: 6 pairs.
Section 2: 7 pairs.
Section 3: Continue section 3 from section 2.
Inner passive and weaver make up this section.
(Refer to page 38, diagrams 61, 62 and 63).

Figure 95

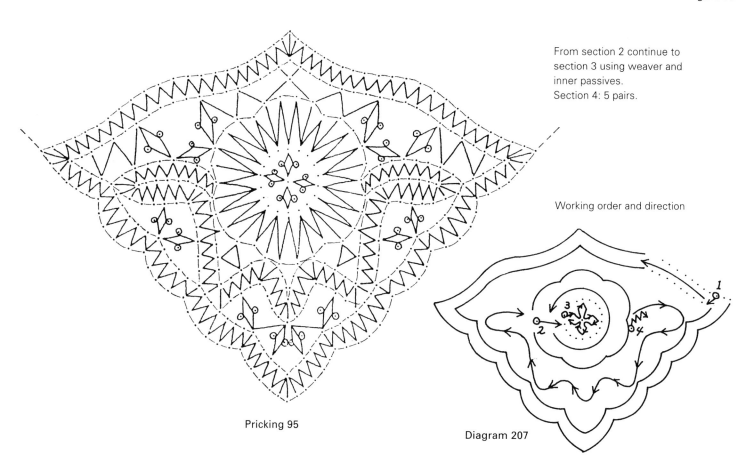

Pricking 95

From section 2 continue to section 3 using weaver and inner passives.
Section 4: 5 pairs.

Working order and direction

Diagram 207

96. Handkerchief Corner-4

Figure 96

Section 1: 8 pairs.
Section 2: 6 pairs.
Section 3: 6 pairs.
Section 4: 6 pairs.
Section 5: 8 pairs.

Working order

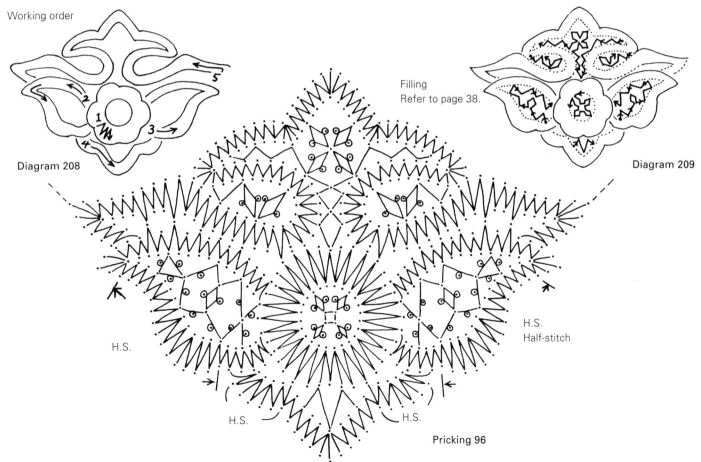

Diagram 208

Filling
Refer to page 38.

Diagram 209

H.S.
Half-stitch

H.S.

H.S.

H.S.

H.S.

Pricking 96

97. Jabot

Section 1
Whole-stitch braid with straight edge.
7 pairs.

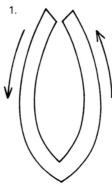

Working order

1.

Diagram 210

Guide to
setting in.

Diagram 211

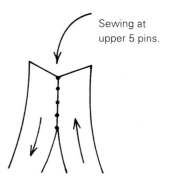

Sewing at
upper 5 pins.

Diagram 212

Pricking 97

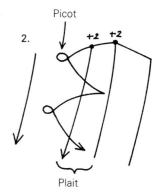

2.

Picot

+2 +2

Plait

Diagram 213

6 pairs.
Whole-stitch braid with straight edge.

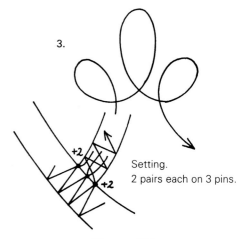

3.

+2

+2

Setting.
2 pairs each on 3 pins.

Diagram 214

Figure 97

4.
Sewing at 4 corners at the cross over.

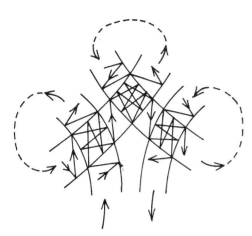

Diagram 215

5.
Direction and filling

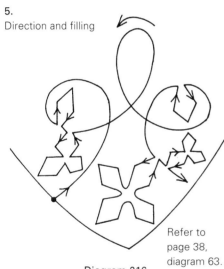

Refer to
page 38,
diagram 63.

Diagram 216

6.
8 pairs

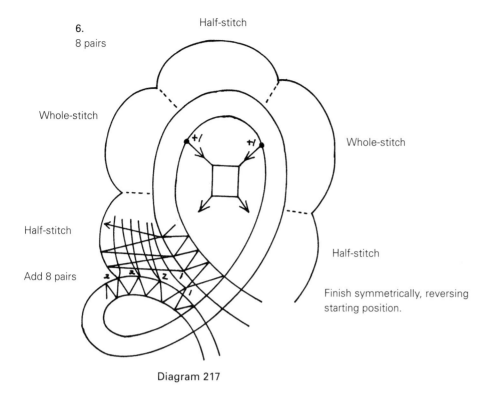

Half-stitch

Whole-stitch

Whole-stitch

Half-stitch

Half-stitch

Add 8 pairs

Finish symmetrically, reversing
starting position.

Diagram 217

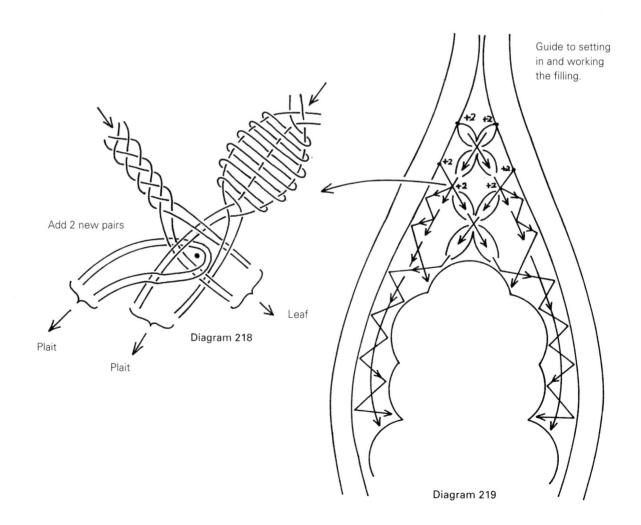

Add 2 new pairs

Leaf

Plait

Plait

Diagram 218

Guide to setting
in and working
the filling.

Diagram 219

98. Ribbon

Outer edge: 5 pairs.
Continuous inner trail: 5 pairs.

For filling bars, make false plaits.
Refer to page 136, diagram 246.

Figure 98a

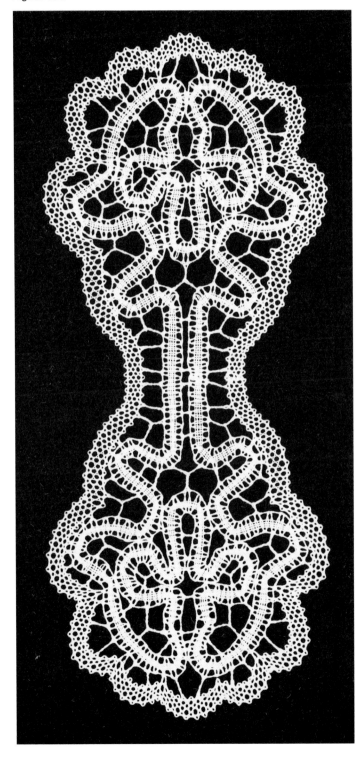

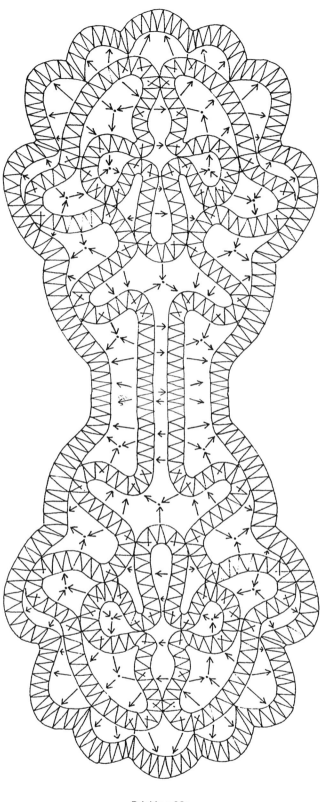

Pricking 98a

Guide to setting in 7 pairs.

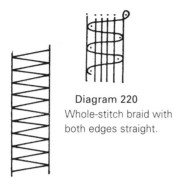

Diagram 220
Whole-stitch braid with
both edges straight.

Pricking 98b (For the braid)

To form the ribbon into a bow, fold
the ribbon in the middle and attach
the short length braid (98b), stitching
into place with needle and thread.

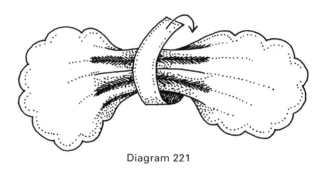

Diagram 221

Figure 98b

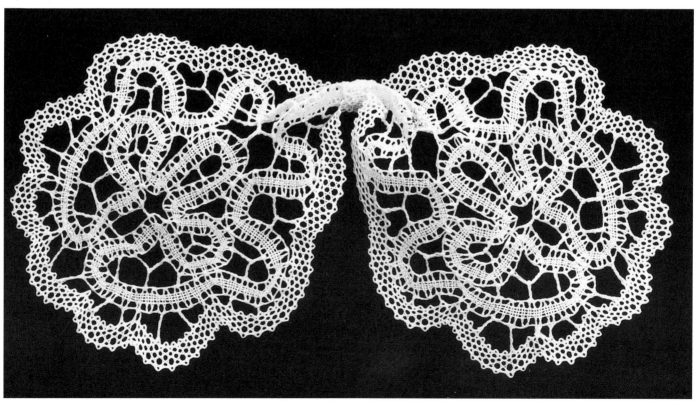

99. Collar-1

Section 1: 7 pairs

Temporary pins

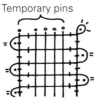

Diagram 222

Guide to setting in and working section 1.

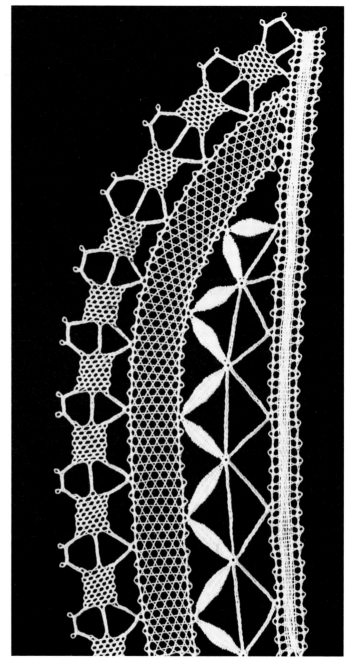

Figure 99

Working order and direction

Pricking 99

Section 2: 8 pairs

H.S
Half-stitch

H.S

Guide to setting in section 2.

Diagram 223

Filling of section 4

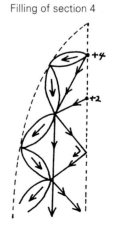

Diagram 224

centre

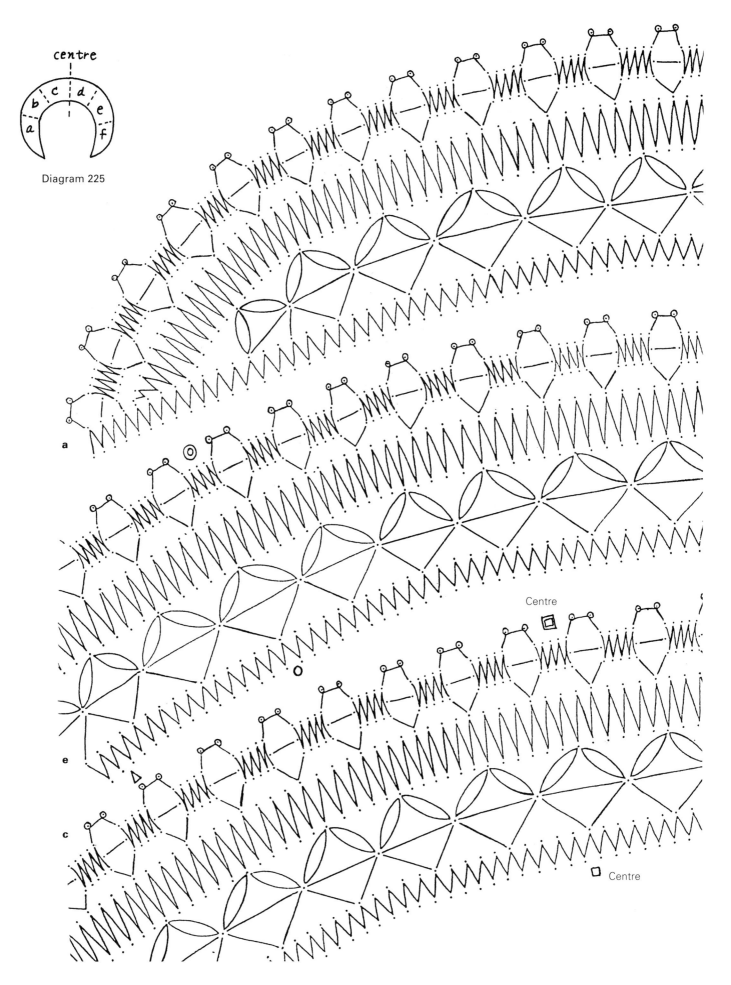

Diagram 225

a

e

c

Centre

Centre

b

f

d

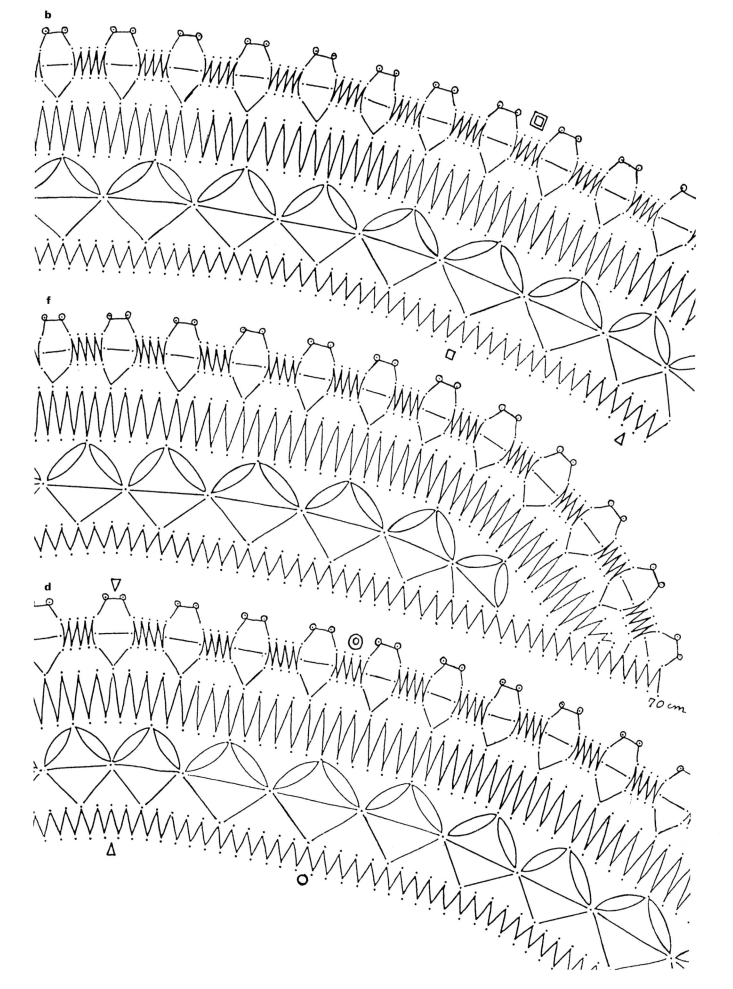

70 cm

129

Figure 99b

Figure 100b

100. Collar-2

7 pairs.

Figure 100a

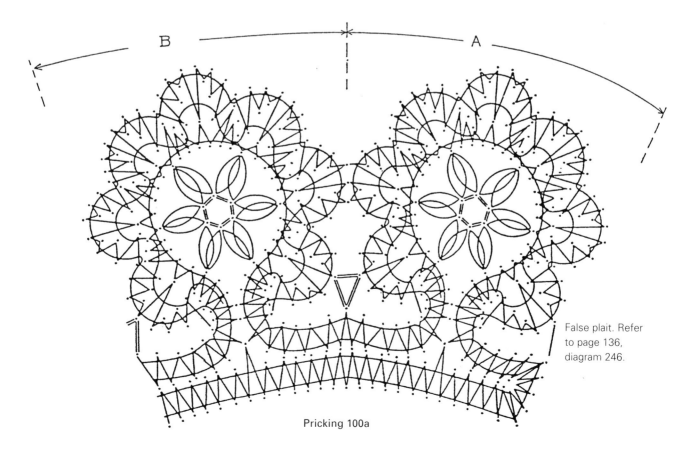

False plait. Refer to page 136, diagram 246.

Pricking 100a

Diagram 226

Make the first leaf and 2nd plait until 7,
then make leaf as arrow 8 until 18.
Use worker and inner passives.

Assemble the whole pattern

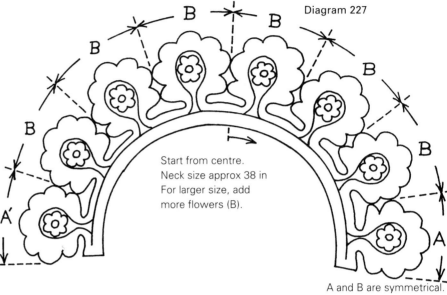

Diagram 227

Start from centre.
Neck size approx 38 in
For larger size, add
more flowers (B).

A and B are symmetrical.

Start from the centre of the neck with 7 pairs.
Refer to page 35, diagram 54.

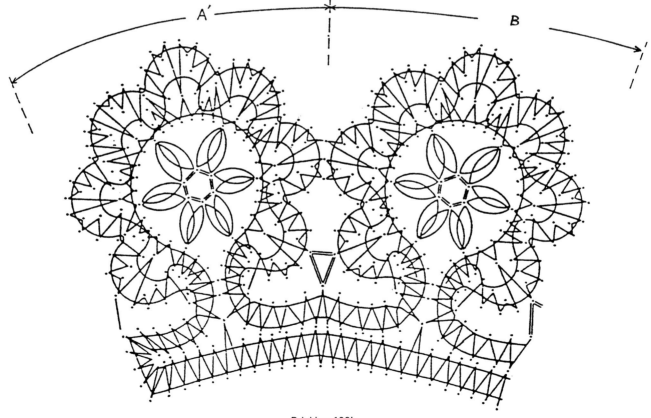

Pricking 100b

Appendix

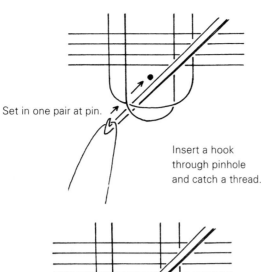

Set in one pair at pin.

Insert a hook through pinhole and catch a thread.

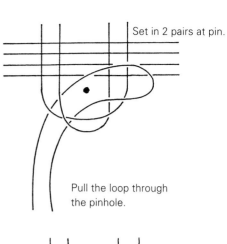

Set in 2 pairs at pin.

Pull the loop through the pinhole.

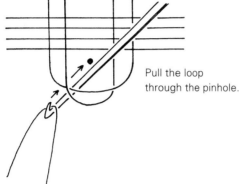

Pull the loop through the pinhole.

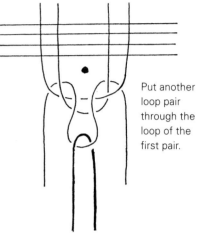

Put another loop pair through the loop of the first pair.

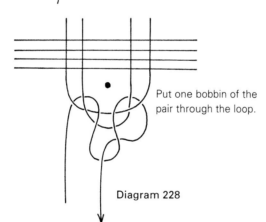

Put one bobbin of the pair through the loop.

Diagram 228

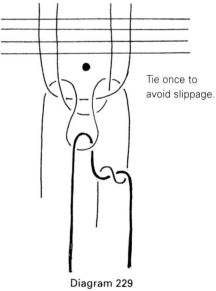

Tie once to avoid slippage.

Diagram 229

Finish: tie reef knots after making final sewings.

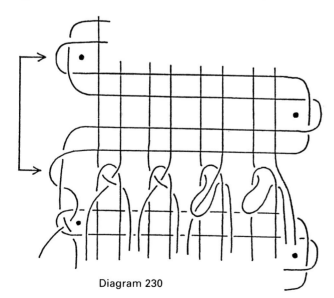

Diagram 230

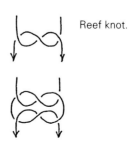

Reef knot.

Diagram 231

Crossing a plait and a single pair.

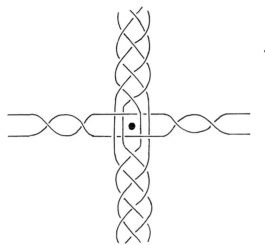

Diagram 232

Windmill crossing: an ingenious method of joining 2 sets of 2 pairs around a pin.

Diagram 233

Crossings using 6 pairs

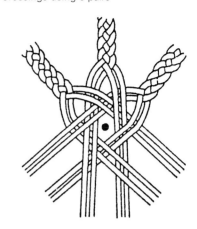

Diagram 235

Leaf

Diagram 236

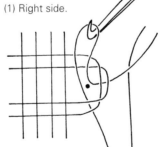
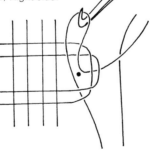

Diagram 234

Hook sewing: a method of sewing and joining. Remove pin, insert hook, catch a thread, pull this thread through pinhole loop. Replace pin.

(1) Right side.

1) Left side.

How to use a mirror.

A clever way to find how your working side will look

Diagram 237

(2) Thread other bobbin through this loop. Replace pin.

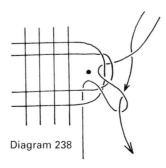

Diagram 238

(2)

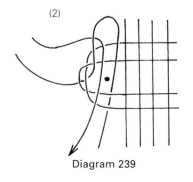

Diagram 239

Add a new pair in whole-stitch braid.

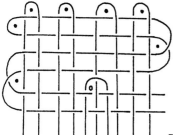

Diagram 240

Take one pair out in whole-stitch braid.

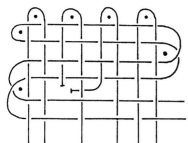

Diagram 241

Knotted picot

Lefthand picot   Righthand picot

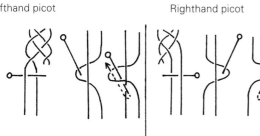

Pull knotted loop to size and pin.

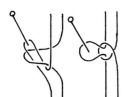

Diagram 244   Diagram 245

Add a new pair in half-stitch braid

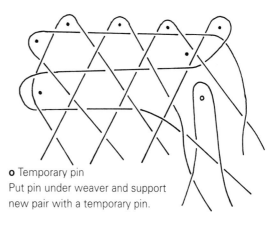

o Temporary pin
Put pin under weaver and support
new pair with a temporary pin.

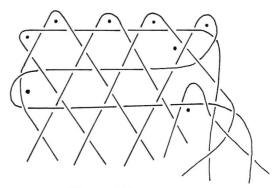

Diagram 242

Take one pair out in half-stitch braid.

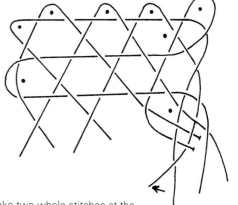

Make two whole-stitches at the
edge and take the second pair out.

Diagram 243

False plait: used to join two sections together with a strong join. Twist worker to form a reasonably tight twist.

Raised sewing

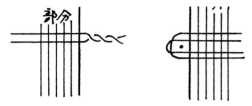

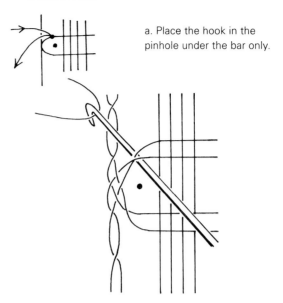

a. Place the hook in the pinhole under the bar only.

a. Sewing into opposite edge.

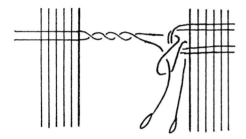

b. On the return, the sewing will be made over the twisted bar.

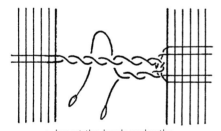

b. Draw a loop from one of the pairs of bobbins.

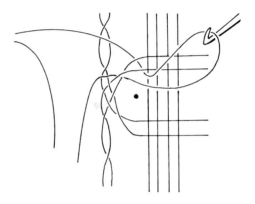

c. Insert the hook under the twisted bar and draw up a loop.

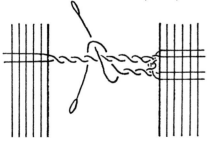

d. Place the other bobbin through a loop.

Diagram 246

c. Pass the other bobbin through the loop and pull up.

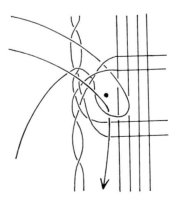

Diagram 247

Pin the lace motif to the material. Take care not to stretch either the lace or the material.

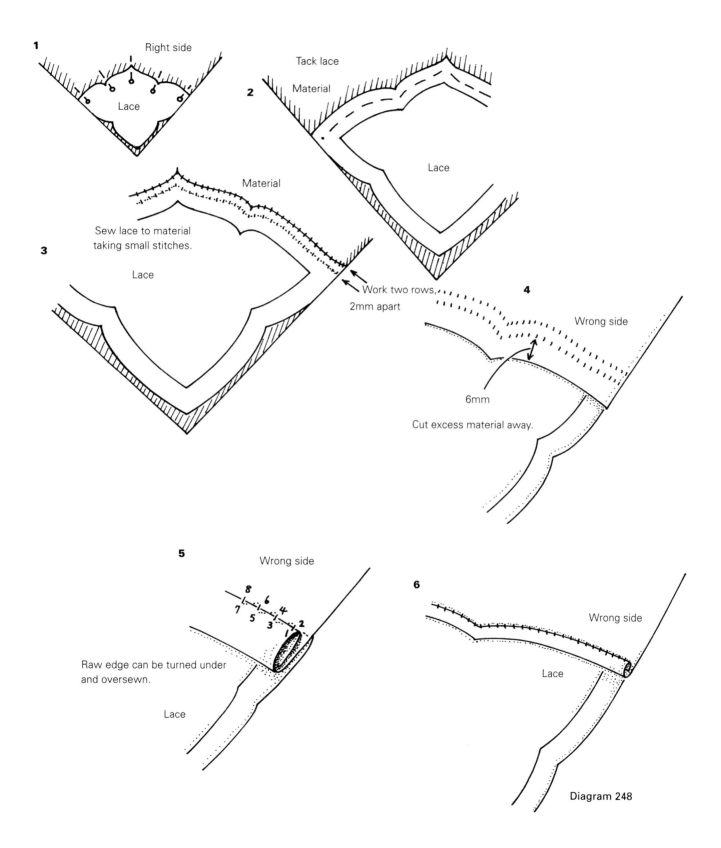

1 Right side
Lace

2 Tack lace
Material
Lace

3 Material
Sew lace to material taking small stitches.
Lace
Work two rows, 2mm apart

4 Wrong side
6mm
Cut excess material away.

5 Wrong side
8 6
7 5 3 4
1 2
Raw edge can be turned under and oversewn.
Lace

6 Wrong side
Lace

Diagram 248

Further Reading

CLAIRE BURKHARD
50 New Bobbin Lace Patterns
(B.T. Batsford Ltd, 1993)

BRIDGET M. COOK
Russian Lace Making
(B.T. Batsford Ltd, 1993)

BRIDGET M. COOK and
ANNA KORABLEVA
Russian Lace Patterns
(B.T. Batsford Ltd, 1996)

GILLIAN DYE
Beginning Bobbin Lace
(First paperback edition,
B.T. Batsford Ltd, 1995)

GHISLAINE EEMANS-MOORS
Rosaline Lace
(B.T. Batsford Ltd, 1996)

ELSIE LUXTON
The Technique Of Honiton Lace
(B.T. Batsford Ltd, 1979)

ELSIE LUXTON
Honiton Lace Patterns
(B.T. Batsford Ltd, 1983)

ELSIE LUXTON and
YUSAI FUKUYAMA
Honiton Lace: The Visual Approach
(B.T. Batsford Ltd, 1988)

ELSIE LUXTON and
YUSAI FUKUYAMA
Royal Honiton Lace
(B.T. Batsford Ltd, 1988)

ELSIE LUXTON and
YUSAI FUKUYAMA
Flowers in Honiton Lace
(B.T. Batsford Ltd, 1992)

MARGARET MAIDMENT
**A Manual of Hand-Made
Bobbin Lace**
(Batsford Ltd, 1931; reprinted by
Piccadilly Rare Books, Paul Minet,
London, 1983

PAMELA NOTTINGHAM
Bedfordshire Lace Making
(B.T. Batsford Ltd, 1992)

PAMELA NOTTINGHAM **The
Technique Of Bobbin Lace**
(B.T. Batsford Ltd, 1976)

Sources of information

United Kingdom

The British College
of Lace
21 Hillmorton Road
Rugby
Warwickshire CV22 5DF

International Old Lacers
Ann Keller
Cool Valley
Abingdon Park
Shankill
Dublin

The Lace Guild
The Hollies
53 Audnam
Stourbridge
West Midlands DY8 4AE

The Lacemakers' Circle
49 Wardwick
Derby DE1 1HY

The Lace Society
Lynwood
Stratford Road
Oversley, Alcester
Warwickshire B49 6PG

Ring of Tatters
Miss B. Netherwood
269 Oregon Way
Chaddesden
Derby DE21 6UR

Australia

Australian Lace Guild
National Committee
Box Hill
Victoria 3128

Australian Lace Magazine
P.O. Box 609
Manly
NSW 2095

Belgium

OIDFA
Lydia Thiels-Mertens
Jagersberg 1
B-3294 Molenstede-Diest

Belgische Kantorganisatie
Irma Boone
Gentse Steenweg 296
B-9240 Zele

France

OIDFA
Suzanne Puech
3 Chemin de Parenty
F-69250 Neuville sur
Saône

Germany

OIDFA
Uta Ulrich
Papenbergweg 33
D-32756 Detmold

Deutscher Klöppelverband
e.V
Schulstr. 38
D-52531 Übach Palenberg

Klöppelschule Nordhalben
Klöppelschule 4
D-96365 Nordhalben

The Netherlands

OIDFA
Elly De Vries
Couwenhoven 52-07
NL-3703 ER Zeist

LOKK
Boterbloem 56
NL-7322 GX Apeldoorn

Switzerland

Fédération de Dentellières
Suisses
Evelyne Lütolf
Buhnstrasse 12
CH-8052 Zürich

USA

OIDFA
Elaine Merritt
5915 Kyburz Place
San José CA 95120
Illinois 60091

International Old Lacers
Box 557
Flanders
NJ 07836

Point Ground Tours &
Publications
124 W. Irvington Place
Denver
Co 80223-1539

OIDFA

(International Bobbin
and Needle
Lace Organization)

President
Lydia Thiels-Mertens
Jagersberg 1
B-3294 Molenstede-Diest
Belgium

Vice President
Alice De Smedt
Welvaartstraat 149
B-Aalst
Belgium

Suppliers

England

BEDFORDSHIRE

Arthur Sells
49 Pedley Lane
Clifton
Shefford SG17 5QT

BERKSHIRE

Chrisken
26 Cedar Drive
Kingsclere RG20 5TD

BUCKINGHAMSHIRE

Bartlett Caesar Partners
The Lace Studio
12 Creslow Court
Galley Hill
Stoney Stratford
Milton Keynes
MK11 1NN

J.S. Sear
Lacecraft Supplies
8 Hillview
Sherington MK16 9NJ

Winslow Bobbins
70 Magpie Way
Winslow MK18 3PZ

SMP Lace
The Lace Workshop
1 Blays, Churchfield Road
Chalfont St Peter SL9 0HB

CAMBRIDGESHIRE

Josie and Jeff Harrison
(*Lace Pillows*)
Walnut Cottage
Winwick
Huntingdon PE17 5PN

Heffers Graphic Shop
(*matt coloured transparent
adhesive film*)
19 Sidney Street
Cambridge CB2 3HL

Spangles, the Bead People
Carole Morris
1 Casburn Lane
Burwell CB5 0ED

CHESHIRE

Lynn Turner (*mail order,
and general supplies*)
Church Meadow Crafts
3 Woodford Lane
over Winsford
CW7 2JS

DEVON

Honiton Lace Shop
44 High Street
Honiton EX14 8PJ

DORSET

Frank Herring & Sons
27 High West Street
Dorchester DT1 1UP

T. Parker (*mail order,
general supplies and bobbins*)
124 Corhampton Road
Boscombe East
Bournemouth BH6 5NZ

ESSEX

Mainly Lace
Moulsham Mill
Parkway
Chelmsford
Essex CM2 7PX

GLOUCESTERSHIRE

Evelyn and Tony Brown
(*Pillow makers*)
Temple Lane Cottage
Littledean
GL14 3NX

Chosen Crafts Centre
46 Winchcombe Street
Cheltenham GL52 2ND

HERTFORDSHIRE

Barleycroft Lacemaking
Supplies, 'Honeypuddle'
13 Barleycroft
Stevenage SG2 9NP

HUMBERSIDE

Sandra's Handpainted
Bobbins
Sandra Fields
31 Seacroft Road
Cleethorpes DN35 0AX

ISLE OF WIGHT

Busy Bobbins
Unit 7
Scarrots Lane
Newport PO30 1JD

KENT

D.J. Hornsby
25 Manwood Avenue
Canterbury CT2 7AH

Francis Iles
73 High Street
Rochester ME1 1LX

MERSEYSIDE

Hayes & Finch
Head Office and Factory
Hanson Road
Aintree
Liverpool L9 9BP

MIDDLESEX

Redburn Crafts
Squires Garden Centre
Halliford Road
Upper Halliford
Shepperton TW17 8RU

NORFOLK

Stitches and Lace
Alby Craft Centre
Cromer Road
Alby
Norwich NR11 7QE

Breklaw Crafts
The Corner Shop
Rickinghall, Diss
IP22 1EG

NORTHAMPTONSHIRE

Anna's Lace Chest
1 Gorse Close
Whitehills
Northants NN2 8ED

Teazle Embroideries
35 Boothferry Road
Hull

STAFFORDSHIRE

John & Jennifer Ford
(*mail order, and lace days only*)
October Hill
Upper Longdon
Rugeley WS15 1QB

SUFFOLK

A.R. Archer (bobbins)
Yew Tree Cottage
High Street
Walsham Le Willows
Bury St Edmunds

Mary Collings (linen by
the metre, and made-up
articles of church linen)
Church Furnishings
St Andrews Hall
Humber Doucy Lane
Ipswich IP4 3BP

Stephen Pearce
Yew Tree Cottage
Chapel Road
Grundisburgh
Woodbridge IP13 6TS

Piper Silks
(specialist silk yarns)
'Chinnery's'
Egremont Street
Glemsford
CO10 7SA

SURREY

Needle and Thread
80 High Street
Horsell
Woking GU21 4SZ

SUSSEX

Southern Handicrafts
20 Kensington Gardens
Brighton BN1 4AC

WARWICKSHIRE

Christine & David Springett
21 Hillmorton Road
Rugby CV22 5DF

WEST MIDLANDS

Acorn Bobbins
Eric Sutton
2 Roman Road
Stoke
Coventry CV2 4LD

Framecraft Miniatures Ltd
372-376 Summer Lane
Hockley
Birmingham B19 3QA

The Needlewoman
21 Needless Alley
off New Street
Birmingham B2 5AE

Stitches
Dovehouse Shopping Parade
335 Warwick Road
Olton, Solihull

YORKSHIRE

The Craft House
22 Bar Street
Scarborough YO11 2HT

Jo Firth
Lace Making &
Needlecraft Supplies
58 Kent Crescent
Lowtown
Pudsey LS28 9EB

Just Lace
Lacemaker Supplies
14 Ashwood Gardens
Gildersome
Leeds LS27 7AS

Sebalace
Waterloo Mill
Howden Road
Silsden BD20 0HA

D.H. Shaw
47 Lamor Crescent
Thrushcroft
Rotherham S66 9QD

Stitchery
6 Finkle Street
Richmond
DL10 4QA

George White
Lacemaking Supplies
40 Heath Drive
Boston Spa LS23 6PB

WILTSHIRE

Doreen Campbell
(frames and mounts)
Highcliff
Bremilham Road
Malmesbury SN16 0DQ

Scotland

Christine Riley
53 Barclay Street
Stonehaven
Kincardineshire

Peter & Beverley Scarlett
Strupak
Hill Head
Cold Wells, Ellon
Grampion

Wales

Bryncraft Bobbins
B.J. Phillips
Pantglas
Cellan
Lampeter
Dyfed SA48 8JD

Hilkar Lace Suppliers
(mail order, and
lace days only)
33 Mysydd Road
Landore
Swansea SA1 2NZ

Australia

Dentelles Lace Supplies
c/o Betty Franks
36 Lang Terrace
Northgate 4013
Brisbane
Queensland

Kipparra Lace Supplies
'Clear Oaks'
Margaret Livingstone
135 Francis Street
Richmond NSW 2753

Lace Craft
Valerie Dunsmore
3 Barton Drive
Mount Eliza
Victoria 3930

Lace Inspirations
Joanne Pope
16 Robertson Road
Leopold
Victoria 3224

J.O. O'Brien
61 Bligh Avenue
Camden
NSW 2570

Annette and John Pollard
1 Panorama Road
Penrith
NSW 2750

Randwick Art and Craft
Supplies
203 Avoca Street
Randwick
NSW 2031

Belgium

't Handwerkhuisje
Katelijnestraat 23
8000 Bruges

Kantcentrum
Peperstraat 3A
8000 Bruges

Manufacture Belge de
Dentelle
6 Galerie de la Reine
Galeries Royales St Hubert
1000 Bruxelles

Orchidée
Mariastraat 18
8000 Bruges

Orchidée N.V.
Fabricage + Groothandel
Blankenbergsesteenweg 65a
8377 Zuienkerke-Brugge

Ann Thys
't Apostelientje
Balstraat 11
8000 Bruges

'Scharlaeken'
J. Vandenweghe
Philipstockstraat 5̄
B-8000

France

La Galerie
Centre d'Enseignement à la
Dentelle Au Fuseau
1 Rue Raphaël
43000 Le Puy en Velay

A L'Econome
Anne-Marie Deydier
Ecole de Dentelle aux
Fuseaux
10 rue Paul Chenavard
69001 Lyon

Rougier et Plé
13-15 bd des Filles de
Calvaire
75003 Paris

Germany

Barbara Fay Verlag &
Versandbuchhandlung
Am Goosberg 2
D-24340 Gammelby

Rittersgrüner
Klöppelboutique
Barbara Neubert
Karlsbader Str. 43
D-08355 Rittersgrün

Werkstatt Textil
Ellen Meyer
An der Obertrave 42
D-23552 Lübeck

The Netherlands

Theo Brejaart
Dordtselaan 146
P.O. Box 5199
3008 AD Rotterdam

Heikina de Rüyter
Zuiderstraat 1
9693 ER Nieuweschans

Magazijn De Vlijt
Lijnmarkt 48
3511 KJ Utrecht

Tiny van Donschot
Dries 95
6006 Al Weert

New Zealand

Peter McLeavey
P.O. Box 69.007
Auckland 8

Switzerland

Buchhandlung
Scheidegger & Co. AG
Obere Bahnhofstr. 10A
CH-8910 Affoltern a.A.

Martin Burkhard
Klöppelzubehör
Jurastrasse 7
CH-5300 Turgi

Fädehax
Irene Solcà
Lolcherstrasse 7
CH-7000 Chur

USA

Arbor House
22 Arbor Lane
Roslyn Heights
NY 11577

Baltazor Fabrics and Lace
3262 Severn Avenue
Metairie
LA 7002-4848

Beggars' Lace
P.O. Box 481223
Denver
CO 80248

Berga Ullman Inc.
P.O. Box 918
North Adams
MA 01247

Forget Me Knot
17828 Bellflower Blvd
Bellflower
CA 90706

Handy Hands
Rt. 1, Box 4
Paxton
Il 6095

Happy Hands
3007 S.W. Marshall
Pendleton
OR 97180

J & R Hensell
P.O. Box 825
Marcola
OR 97454-0825

International Old Lacers Inc.
124 West Irvington Place
Denver
CO 80223-1539

The Lacemaker
176 Sunset Ave S.
P.O. Box 77525
Edmonds
WA 98177-525

Lacis
3163 Adeline Street
Berkeley
CA 94703

Laurik's Lacemaking
Supplies
3790 El Camino Real Suite
103
Palo Alto
CA 94306

Robin's Bobbins
RT1 Box 1736
Mineral Bluff
GA 30559-9736

Robin and Russ
Handweavers
533 North Adams Street
McMinnville
OR 97128

Snowgoose
1880
S. Pierce 4
Lakewood
CO 80232

Unicorn Books
Glimakra Looms 'n
Yarns Inc.
1304 Scott Street
Petaluma
CA 94954-1181

Unique Apparel
6501 E 113th Street
Kansas City
MO 64134

The Unique and
Art Lace Cleaners
5926 Delman Boulevard
St Louis
MO 63112

Van Sciver Bobbin Lace
130 Cascadilla Park
Ithaca
NY 14850

The World in Stitches
82 South Street
Milford
NR 03055